LIFE 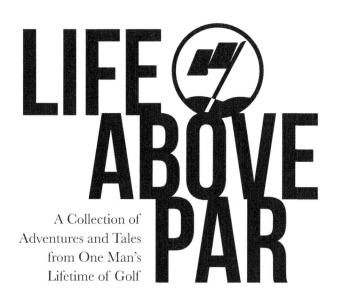 ABOVE PAR

A Collection of
Adventures and Tales
from One Man's
Lifetime of Golf

Phillip A. Robinson Jr.

ISBN: 979-8-9880917-0-7 (paperback)
ISBN: 979-8-9880917-1-4 (ebook)

Cover Design by Berge Design
Photo Credit for front and back covers:
Front: Laura Nicholas: Picture taken at Highland Links, North Truro, MA
Back: Mark Robinson: Picture taken at Old Head Golf Links, Kinsale, Ireland

Dedicated to the three brightest lights in my life,

My wife Tina
And my boys
Erik and Kurt

Blessed!

CONTENTS

AUTHOR'S NOTE

This book is a project I have wanted to tackle for a long time. The first two years of my retirement offered the perfect opportunity to write it. I have told these stories to people over the years and thought it would be a worthwhile challenge to collect them all in one place.

The events and stories told in this book are as I remember them. If there are any inaccuracies in what I have written, they are the result of the passage of time and my aging memory of the events. Some of these events happened many years ago, but I believe what I have written is an accurate description of what took place.

In a few cases I added dialogue and did my best to recreate what was said. There could be cases where I took literary license as part of telling these stories. In some cases, I have left out names of individuals who are part of the stories. In most instances, they are people who I have lost contact with and have no way to find them to ask their permission to be included in the book.

I have enjoyed reading the works of many fine golf writers: Tom Coyne, George Peper, Michael Bamberger, James Dodson, and my high school classmate Jim McCabe to name a few. Their styles and storytelling abilities inspired me to give writing a try. Unlike them, I am not a professional, just a regular guy who has been fortunate to have many great golf memories to write about.

My book is set up like a round of golf. There are eighteen holes, a front and back nine, a halfway house, and a 19th hole. There is also an appendix with a few extra stories, including the one that started this project, my guide to successful business golf. Hole #1 tells the story of how I got started in golf and the balance are stories about my adventures. Some stories are comical, some are serious and there are even a couple about love.

I mention in the book that both my sons received scholarships from the Francis Ouimet Scholarship Fund. Our family has participated in the Ouimet Bag Tag fundraising program at our golf club, and we have attended the annual banquet on several occasions. If the book does well, I would love to donate a portion of the profits to the Ouimet Fund so others will continue to benefit from the outstanding work they do.

Maybe my parents knew something years ago when they named me Phillip Allan Robinson and gifted me with the perfect golfer initials, PAR. I have been chasing par now for sixty years and look forward to doing it for many more.

I hope you enjoy reading these stories as much as I enjoyed experiencing them!

FORWARD

Finding true love can be as rare as experiencing a hole-in-one. With my husband Phil, I've been lucky enough to have found both.

For us, golf is much more than a sport. It is an activity that spans generations, bringing family and friends together with a common goal… avoiding the sand traps! Golf teaches patience, requires practice, provides ups (birdies) and downs (double bogeys), but also great excitement. Golf, like life, holds endless possibilities.

I hope you enjoy these tales from the fairway (and the 19th hole), and good luck in your quest for life's holes-in-one!

From a willing golf widow, golf partner, and loving wife,
Tina Robinson

THE FRONT 9

Hole #1

IN THE BEGINNING

Everyone has a story about how they got started playing the great game of golf. The following is how my lifelong journey in golf began. My thanks to all who have played a part. It has been an amazing adventure and I know there are more fun memories to come. I hope you will take a moment to think about the start of your golf journey while you read about mine.

* * *

There was no time or place for golf in my young life. Somehow, golf found a way in.

I grew up in North Quincy, MA in an idyllic neighborhood on North Bayfield Road. It was a wonderful place to grow up because our neighborhood was a "block" or circle with a north and south side. There were plenty of families with an abundance of kids. Our lives in the summer revolved around Wollaston Beach that was walkable from our homes. When the tide was in, we were at the beach, and when it was out, we played baseball or rode our bikes. We went everywhere on our bikes, sometimes farther away than we would ever let on to our parents.

In the other seasons, it was football, basketball, hockey and even street hockey. All were the games we loved as kids.

We played all different kinds of football, from tackle football in the sand on the beach, to touch football out on our street. We even traveled to other fields to play tackle football games against other neighborhoods. No parents involved, just kids playing against other kids. These games were always something I looked forward to, and I would sit in class and daydream about what game we would be playing after school.

As kids, we were never allowed to sit home, and we always figured out something to do to pass the time. Playing these sports taught us great life lessons. We learned to get along and settle disputes and arguments without a parent telling us what to do. Conflict resolution was sometimes not easy. In the end, we figured it out. We had to if we wanted to keep on playing, and it forced us to learn the fine art of compromise.

My earliest memory on how golf found a wedge into all of this started with my grandfather Albert Robinson and my dad, Phil Robinson.

The first time I remember a conversation about golf in our family was a day when we were heading to visit my grandparents after dinner one summer evening in 1965. On the way to their home, we passed Wollaston Golf Club, then, a private club in Quincy, MA. On this night we could barely make the left turn from West Squantum Street on to Harvard Street to get to their house. Cars were parked on the sides of both roads and were parked as far as I could see.

When we arrived my dad asked my grandfather if he knew what was going on at Wollaston. My grandfather told us that the most popular golfer in the country, Arnold Palmer, was playing at Wollaston. Palmer was playing an exhibition match that day with rising star "Champagne" Tony Lema. Lema won the British Open in 1964 at St Andrews and five other tournaments that year. Lema got the unique nickname by buying the press "bubbly" to celebrate his wins. Tragically, Lema and his wife passed away two years after his British Open win in a plane crash.

My grandparents lived a short distance from Wollaston on Exeter Street. Their house had a large basement full of many interesting items. Some of those items were a collection of paintings, antique pistols that I enjoyed playing cowboy with (no bullets), a wood working shop my dad and grandfather loved to work in and lastly a mismatched set of old golf clubs.

Their house had a large and long backyard and a comfortable screened in porch. One night later in the summer when we came over to visit, the clubs had made their way out from the basement and my grandfather Albert was hitting whiffle golf balls across the backyard. My dad joined in, and I can remember the balls bouncing off the screens on the porch and landing without causing any damage.

They both hit balls for a time and when they were done, my reward for shagging balls for them was a couple of swings with the clubs. The clubs were big for me, but I do remember it not being as easy as it looked when the adults were taking swings. I wanted to keep swinging but the mosquitoes started biting voraciously and it was time to head inside to the safety of the screened in porch.

My grandparents moved to Maine and the set of golf clubs moved from their basement to ours. The clubs sat dormant for a time, but one summer shortly after the clubs moved in with us, I had the chance to learn how to use them thanks to the Quincy Recreation Department.

Quincy Rec had multiple program offerings for kids year-round. In the summer, each park in the city was staffed by a male and female councilor and had daily activities and sports. In addition to this there were specialty offerings including swimming, rowing, sailing, and golf lessons. These programs were free and the only requirement for the specialty programs was you had to find your way to the site they were offered. Since we did everything on our bikes, this was no problem for my group of friends.

We learned that Quincy Rec taught golf once a week at Montclair Field about two miles from our street. We all thought it would be fun to try golf, so we signed up and biked over for our lessons. What kept us engaged was once the instructors thought we were skilled enough, we would be allowed on a Monday to play golf on a "real" golf course. The free golf would be at Furnace Brook Golf Course, a nine-hole course also in Quincy.

The class of golfers was small and after a month of once-a-week lessons we got the OK to head to Furnace Brook the following Monday. The tee time was early, and we needed to convince our parents to give us a ride over and back. Carrying the clubs and riding our bikes would not be a good match. We got our ride to and from the course set up and arrived to meet our chaperone and teacher for the day.

Our guy was an experienced golfer and was supposed to school us on the finer points of proper course etiquette. Things went so well (not really!), that after we played four holes our chaperone abandoned us! We waited on the 4th tee for him for a long time, but he had disappeared. The group behind us was getting close, so we moved on and finished the last five holes on our own.

Looking back, I am sure our chaperone was frustrated with our level of play and just had enough. He must have let somebody know about our skill level because that was the last time, we were invited to play Furnace Brook that summer. I cannot say I blame them.

Speaking of Furnace Brook Golf Course, it was a special place for me. Furnace Brook was special because it was a place where a number of firsts in my life happened.

The first time I played golf on a real course was at Furnace Brook.

The first hole at "The Brook" uniquely served as a ski slope in the winter. It was called Heavenly Hill. It only had a small rope tow, but it was a perfect place to learn how to ski. It was the first slope I ever skied down and the place I learned to ski. My family and I skied there many times and often on nights during high school.

Heavenly Hill was the place I met my first serious girlfriend. Her family owned a house at the bottom of the hill right next to the first green. We met on the slopes at Heavenly Hill and enjoyed both skiing and golf together.

Later on in life, my brother Mark would become a Furnace Brook member and club President. With Mark, I played my first member/guest tournament at Furnace Brook. Lots of history with our family on that piece of land.

Furnace Brook was my first shot at playing for real, and I had the bug. Later that summer our family took our annual vacation to Ogunquit, ME. I convinced my parents that there needed to be room in our car for the golf clubs.

I knew there was a 9-hole course near our house and was hoping we could find a way to play it.

Late one afternoon my dad decided that we would head over to the course, Cape Neddick Country Club, to play nine holes. My dad knew the course would be less busy late in the afternoon and there was a better chance they would allow us to play. My bike had come along on this trip too, and I had ridden down the narrow winding road over to Cape Neddick a number of times to scout out the course and holes.

We headed over to the course and my excitement level was through the roof. That excitement was tempered quickly when we entered the pro shop and the man behind the counter took a long hard stare at me. The kind of stare you could feel. I could tell right away he was not happy to see us, and his greeting was icy cold.

With a condescending tone in his voice, he asked how old I was. I said eleven. He looked at my dad and said to him, "sorry, your son is too young to be allowed out on this golf course. Nobody under fourteen is allowed to play." My dad pushed back and pointed out that there was nobody playing, and the course looked empty. The counterman's response was, "rules are the rules, I am sorry, but he is too young." He added an extra little dagger by saying "you both need to have your own golf bag and clubs to play anyway. Since you only have one bag and set of clubs, I could not let you play even if he were old enough."

I was crushed.

My parents were disappointed too, but they found a workable solution a day or so later. We found another course, Dutch Elm Golf Course a little further north from

Ogunquit in Arundel, ME that had no such restrictions. It was a golf course surrounded by a corn field. Thankfully, they were willing to take our money and did not care if we used clubs from the same bag or how old I was. It was hot and not busy. I cannot remember how many holes we played but I do remember being happy to be out playing even in the heat.

Life always works in interesting ways and the next summer brought on my full indoctrination into the golf world. I was in sixth grade and the neighborhood kids were finding odd jobs to make a little money. My neighbor and friend Joey Joyce had recently become a caddie at Wollaston Golf Club. Joey told me Wollaston was looking for a few more caddies, and next thing I knew I was signed up for the caddie school. This school would help me learn the finer points about the game of golf.

I had much to learn, and the first lesson was to track your golfer's shot and know where the ball ended up. Our class struggled with this assignment and when our instructor hit his first shot of our training, nobody had any idea where it had gone. The instructor glared at our group and told us we better get with it, if we wanted to be caddies.

After his warning, we all improved with each class, and we completed the six training lessons. Now, I would need to show up at the course, sit on the caddie bench and wait my turn to be chosen to carry a member's bag for a round. The caddiemaster had to get used to seeing you and there was definitely a ranking system in place. New caddies got the members that paid the least and played the worst. There was much sitting around and waiting but my friends told me to hang in because it was the only way you would finally start getting loops. You did not make any money, till you got a loop.

I will never forget my first day. I sat all day on the caddie bench and waited for a chance. That chance came late in the day when a member showed up and wanted to get some practice in. I was the last caddie on the bench still waiting for work. I recognized the member. He was the owner of our local Dairy Queen, which my family was a frequent customer of during the summer months.

This day, I would not be going out on the course but would be performing another caddie duty, "shagging" golf balls. Since Wollaston had no practice range, members who wanted to practice would stand on a tee above the 16th and 17th fairways and hit balls across them. The member would motion you in or out as he was aiming at you. The object for the caddie was to catch the ball quickly, pop it back into the shag bag, and then sprint back to the original position to be ready for the next shot. It was like being a human flag stick!

I was happy to get the chance and by the end was covered in sweat from sprinting back and forth in the warm summer heat. For my hours' worth of "shagging" I received the royal sum of $2.50. About the time I finished, my parents showed up, since I had been gone from our house for over 12 hours. I proudly displayed the first money I had ever earned and could not wait to get back the next day to do it again.

Being a caddie was key in my learning about the game. I learned skills I still use today in how to find balls and mark the direction that offline shots travel. I certainly learned the rules and saw some incredibly good golf and some awful golf. The best benefit though of being a caddie, besides the money, was caddie golf Monday.

Each Monday Wollaston was closed to members but open to the caddies to play golf. The closest public golf course to us was Ponkapoag in Canton and there was no way we could ride our bikes there. This was an opportunity to play the game on a regular basis and improve.

My mismatched set of clubs got regular work in, and I learned much about how to get around the course. I certainly learned that the game was hard but good shots were so much fun and as everyone who plays knows, the good shots keep you coming back.

I learned the hard way that there were caddies who were skillful players and were more than happy to sucker you into a match and take your hard earned money. I quickly figured out that these were guys I was not ready to play with.

Sadly, for me, Wollaston Golf Club was growing and needed more space to add a pool and other amenities. There was no room to grow at the current location as it was surrounded by houses and roads. The club was able to purchase a large parcel of farmland in the adjacent town of Milton and was building a new course. The new location would not be in walking or biking distance from my home, so my days being a caddie ended earlier than I had wanted.

This change did put a crimp in my playing, but golf did always find a way in right through high school. A few times a year a group of friends would get together and make the pilgrimage over to Ponkapoag for a couple of rounds. I always looked forward to playing and would go every chance I could get.

It took a couple of years, but the old Wollaston site underwent a remake and came back with a fresh look and new name. The "new" golf course was called Presidents Golf Course and it was open to the public. It was named this because two Quincy residents, John Adams and John Quincy Adams were Presidents of the United States.

For me, college was the time in life when my interest in golf took off.

I attended Nichols College in Dudley, MA. At the time, Nichols was a smaller sized business school which happened to have a championship caliber football team. When I went on my football recruiting visit, I noticed something that caught my interest. It had nothing to do with classes, majors, or football. What excited me was the school had a nine-hole golf course that was across the street from our athletic fields.

At the end of the visit, I inquired about the course. It turned out, college students could be members for a minimal amount of money. If I had any doubt about attending Nichols, this sealed the deal for me. Quite a way to make a large life decision!

Once I arrived at school I could not wait to head over to the course and play. One slight issue though, I was a football player and our double session practices went on for the first two weeks we were at school. Every day from our practice field I could see the course, but with two practices a day there was no time or energy for golf.

Finally, after our first inter-squad scrimmage and a week of grueling two a day practices, our coach, "Iron" Mike Vendetti, gave us a day off. Most of my teammates headed home for a day (they had cars, I did not) and a few headed down to Webster Lake to enjoy the beach and a swim. Not me though; I grabbed my old, mismatched set of clubs and set off on a hike across campus and our playing fields to the Nichols College Golf Course. My teammates would have thought I was nuts if they knew what I was doing, but I could not have been happier to go play.

After being informed by a group of members that I was starting on the third hole and not the first, I made my first tour around the Nichols 9. It was blazing hot, but it was a good diversion after a week of taking a beating at football practice. I knew one thing for sure, this would not be the last time I played the course.

Football did not leave much time for golf in the fall, but once in a while I would sneak over for a Sunday nine. Likely my coaches would not have been happy, but it was my only day off and I really enjoyed playing.

I got a tremendous amount of use out of the golf course during my four years at Nichols. I found a group that would go over and play at the drop of a hat. A number of my teammates played golf too. My football friends Larry Bean, Billy Fraser, Bob Wotton, and my roommate Gary Cascio would head over to the course any afternoon or sometimes in the spring after dinner.

We had one accomplished player in our group, Mike Villanova. Mike was not a football player (he did take films of all our games) but was an excellent golfer.

Mike played high school golf, won a state championship and was a member of the Nichols College golf team. Mike gave me my first real lesson in golf, and it was simple. I had a habit of standing over the ball for an exceedingly long time, thinking about all the things I had read I should be doing from my golf instruction books. Finally, Mike could not take it anymore and one day implored me to, "just get up and hit the damn ball!" It was great advice that I still use to this day.

Playing at school stoked my passion for the game. I bought my first pair of golf shoes and replaced my mismatched set of clubs with my first new set of clubs (Spaulding Elite woods and irons bought from Herman's Sporting Goods). I broke 50 and 90 for the first time ever there and had my first Eagle on the then par four, 7th, hole (it is now the 5th hole).

After I graduated from Nichols, and secured my first job, my obsession with golf continued. I was lucky to have a flexible schedule and spent significant time practicing at Presidents Golf Club and any driving range I could find on the South Shore of Boston. I knew the location of every range south of the city and hit balls at every one of them. Some days even in my work clothes!

It helped that I had a group of friends at home in Quincy who all played. We would play sometimes on Friday afternoons (skipping out on work) and every weekend. We started taking golf trips and playing in local charity tournaments. My first job had a golf league and I joined that and played every Tuesday night. Golf filled that competitive void that all the other sports had filled for years.

All this led to the stories I have accumulated through the subsequent years of playing golf. Those stories are shared on the following pages. I hope you have as much fun reading the stories as I had experiencing them!

Hole #2

BEAT THE PRO

The 70's and 80's were the hay days of local Boston news on television. The six and eleven o'clock news was must see TV in those days. It was pre-CNN and ESPN, and the TV news was the only way to catch up to what was going on in the world.

In Boston, there were three choices for news, Channels 4, 5, and 7. Channels 4 and 5 were always the ratings front runners and Channel 7 brought up the rear. The stations followed the same format in their broadcast with news coming first, weather second, and sports last.

Each station had their star anchors. Channel 4 with Tom Ellis and Tony Pepper followed in later years by Liz Walker and Jack Williams. Channel 5 had the husband-and-wife team of Natalie Jacobson and Chet Curtis. Chet and Nat were a Boston power couple, and no doubt Natalie was beloved and the most popular news figure in Boston.

Each station had a star meteorologist. Dick Albert was on Channel 5, Bruce Schwegler on Channel 4 and Harvey Leonard on 7. Each had their own style, and all tried to make the weather more fun and interesting.

Last but certainly not least, was sports.

It was a time when all games were not on TV and many times the only highlights you would get would be on the

11pm news. My wife Tina always tells the story of going to Celtics games in the Larry Bird era and rushing home after the game to catch the highlights on the 11pm news.

The three sports anchors competed hard to get scoops on the local sports scene. They all had distinct personalities and those personalities came across in the way they covered the Boston sports scene.

John Dennis was the guy on Channel 7. Dennis was serious, and a straight shooter. Dennis went on to a long and successful career in sports talk radio in the mornings on the original sports talk station in Boston, WEEI.

Channel 5 had the local guy, Mike Lynch, who went to Swampscott High and then on to be the place kicker for Harvard. "Lynchie" came across as a good guy and always brought local flavor to his broadcasts. He made a nice niche for himself with coverage of local high school sports with his High Five Awards and Thanksgiving Night wrap up of the traditional high school Turkey Day football rivalry games.

Lastly, was Bob Lobel of WBZ Channel 4. To me, Lobel was the most popular of the three and his irreverent style endeared him to his viewers. Certainly, one of his more memorable lines always took place when a Boston team traded away a player. When the player returned to play against the hometown teams and made a good play or had a good game, Lobel would always quip, "why can't we get players like that?" My wife Tina and I still say this line to each other to this day.

While Mike Lynch took an interest in high school sports, Lobel was an avid golfer. Back around 1990 to promote his interest in golf, Channel 4 started a golf show called Beat the Pro.

The show would run late Sunday night and the concept was straightforward. The WBZ staff would pick a local golf course to feature, and they would visit the course with a Boston sports celebrity during the week and hit shots on a par 3 hole. The shots by the pro would be measured and the closest one to the hole would be the target for the field to shoot for on the weekend. For a small donation to charity, each person who played the hole at the chosen course that weekend, would have the chance to "Beat the Pro."

If you beat the pro, you received Beat the Pro logo golf balls. If you were closest to the pin for the day, you received pro shop credit and an invite to the championship shootout. At the shootout, you would compete with the other weekly winners for valuable prizes including a golf trip to Florida, a large color TV, a high-priced watch and first-class round-trip airline tickets for any destination in the United States.

Luckily, in the first year of the show I happened to be playing at Falmouth Country Club on the day Channel 4 was filming. In these days, it was unusual for me to be play-ing on a weekend. A friend who had a house on a lake in Mashpee was having a summer cookout and all my golfing friends with their wives and children would be attending. The wives and children would be spending the day at the lake swimming while we headed off to play golf. A perfect situation for me.

As we started our round, we noticed in the parking lot a camera crew getting ready to head out on to the course. At this point we were not sure what they were doing, but we found out a short time later when our group arrived at the short par 3 4th hole.

As we approached the 4th hole, play was backed up and the group in front of us was still on the tee. The camera crew we saw in the parking lot had arrived at the tee and we learned the Beat the Pro filming was about to start. It took a couple minutes for the crew to get set up, and the group on the tee wanted a chance to participate.

The pro to beat that day was Johnny Rembert. Rembert was a New England Patriot linebacker who attended Clemson University and had a ten-year pro career from 1983 through 1993. Rembert appeared in the 1985 Super Bowl, and he was a two time All Pro. Rembert had a good swing, a funky looking good luck hat, and his best shot was sixteen feet from the hole. That would be the shot for us to beat.

Things got rolling and the group in front of us hit up to the green without any quality shots. After a short wait for them to finish out the hole, we were on the tee.

I was playing with friends Tom Donovan, Paul Hanlon, and Paul's work friend George Lowery. We were having our normal match and it was always a good one. Participating in Beat the Pro was unexpected and was icing on the cake of what was already a great day.

When it was our turn to play, the group behind us pulled up to the tee. This foursome was the second of our group of friends playing that day. With them now catching up to us, we were going to have a rowdy audience on the tee.

The camera was now rolling, and we all had the chance for glory. I hit last and hit a pitching wedge to the hole that was playing 120 yards. As soon as I hit the shot, I knew it was going to be good. I gave the shot a "get close" shout.

My friends were roaring too, and as we watched the shot, it never left the stick. The shot was hit high and stopped two feet six inches from the hole. The ball almost went in on the fly!

For the record (as I know many will ask), I made the putt for birdie!

The good news was I had beaten the pro. The bad news was we were group number two of the day and the camera crew planned on taping shots for another five hours. Plenty more golfers would have their chance to knock it inside my shot.

We went on to finish our round, but it was hard to stop thinking about what had just happened. The whole thing was like an out of body experience. Before we left the course, we were able to find out that my shot had held up through the day and the crew was getting close to having enough tape. I knew then there would only be a few more groups with a chance to beat me.

The news came later that day that I had won. It was exciting, and we had a victory celebration at the cookout.

More details would be coming about the finals due to the Falmouth show being only the second of the summer season. The producer told me the filming of the shows would go on for ten more weeks. He also let me know he would be in touch and that this episode would air the following Sunday.

There was much anticipation from friends and family about my upcoming appearance on TV. I wondered what the tape would look like and how my swing would look on camera.

The big night came, and our VCR was set to record the event. First, Lobel did a brief overview about the club and course. Next was his interview with Johnny Rembert and video of Rembert hitting his shots.

The funny part came next, when they showed a string of bloopers; shots going sideways, shots going into the water, and into the woods. I remember the camera caught one guy fishing balls out of the water with his ball retriever! The bad shots were funny with Lobel narrating and making sarcastic comments about each person and their inept results. Lobel clearly enjoyed this part of the show.

Finally, at the end of the show, the big moment came with Lobel showing my winning shot and announcing my name. It was exciting to see the swing and shot and hear the strike of the ball. You could hear my group of friends in the background yelling and cheering as the shot looked better and better, until it settled close to the hole. It was fun, and I did earn enough pro shop credit for winning closest to the pin to get a couple of shirts and a sweater from Falmouth Country Club.

It is a pity the story did not end here.

I now had ten weeks to think about the final and think about it I did. Morning, noon, and night to the point I drove everyone around me nuts. While I had played quite a few matches and member guest tournaments, I had never been in something where big money prizes were at stake, and it would all be on TV. I could not shake the thought of the prizes and I even lost sleep thinking about them.

Since I was an early winner, I had the chance to watch all the other shows and winners. After watching them all, at least in my mind, I was the best golfer and lowest handicap of the group. This knowledge was not a good thing. My expectations for winning big were building.

Finally, Fall arrived and so did the date for the final. It would be at Sterling Country Club in Sterling, MA. It was a long way from Sandwich, MA where I was living, and at a course I had never played.

About a week before the finals, my friend Tom Donovan and I headed out to Sterling to play the course and check out the 16th hole, the hole the final would use. I was able to hit some extra shots from the 16th white tee box to get a feel for the distance and club I would use on the big day. The hole was a steep downhill hole playing 150 yards. I was glad to get to play it before the final. Since it was an all-male final, we figured WBZ would use the white tees. That assumption proved to be one of the numerous things that would go wrong the day of the final.

The big day arrived, and we had to be up early to get out to Sterling on time. I wanted to have plenty of time to warm up and stretch and be ready to take home the grand prize.

To add to the pressure of the day, I had a work trip planned and would have to fly to Chicago after the event. This work trip would be important for me. It was a high-profile project that with success could change my career and career path. With these two events happening at the same time, I had much on my mind when we got into the car to start the day.

Even though I had made a reconnaissance trip to Sterling, we managed to get lost on the way out. All of a sudden, my cushion of time was evaporating, stress was building and then the unthinkable happened.

A Massachusetts State Trooper was set up for a speed trap on a blind downhill section of the highway and I was pulled over and given a ticket for speeding. It is never a quick process. I tried to explain to the trooper why I was going faster than normal, but I do not think it helped. It may have made things worse. At this point I thought for sure I would miss the event.

We arrived right at the starting time at 10 am, but luckily for me the camera crew was late. Thankfully, there would be time for me to warm up. Finally, a good break I thought to myself.

I ran up to the range quickly to hit a few balls. The first swing was a little tight and was a worm burner, a ground ball. The second one was worse, a shank dribbling down the right front of the range by a couple of my competitors. I drew some interesting looks from the others on the range. I hit another shot that was a little better, but I could see it was hit close to the heel of the club. Another near shank.

This was not what I needed right now; my swing was deserting me. The warmup session ended mercifully after ten balls, as they were now calling for us to head out on to the course. None of the shots on the range were hit well and I was not brimming with confidence when I headed to the 16th hole.

We drove out to the hole and there were many friends and family members gathered to watch the contest. We all congregated on the tee and our host, Mr. Lobel, gave us our instructions.

The group would be divided in half and before we hit, Lobel would conduct a brief interview with each of us. Then each player would hit their three shots with only the one closest to the hole counting for the prizes. After the first group hit, the process would be repeated with the second half of the field. I was in the second half of the field.

About this time, I recognized another surprise. We would be hitting from the most forward tees on the hole. So much for the trip out to practice and get a feel for the shot! The hole would play about thirty yards shorter than I thought when we practiced the prior week.

Lobel was good at making us all feel comfortable. His questions were basic and easy to answer. Still with the camera rolling you could tell everyone was nervous. Then it was our time to get down to business and hit our shots. Nobody in the first group hit it close and even with my bad warm up I was eager to hit one in tight.

Our group was up, and my turn would be in the middle of our group. I would have a good idea about how the others had done by hitting so late in the competition. Before I knew it, I was being motioned over by the producer for my turn. That is when the fun really began.

When I was getting ready to hit my first shot, my two-year-old son Erik escaped from his mother and sprinted down to the tee to see what I was doing. It was a natural reaction for him because I took Erik to the driving range all the time to hit balls. He loved going to the range and when he saw me hitting balls, I am sure he wanted to hit some balls too.

Lobel was all over this and had a blast asking Erik questions and getting his comments while I was getting ready to hit my first shot. The shot was long, and Erik asked me "what are you doing dad?" I growled under my breath that I was trying to hit one closer to the flag than that.

Now years later, it is all funny, but it was not so funny when it was going on. My second shot was not much better and missed to the right, a long way from the hole. Lobel kept asking Erik questions and was having fun interviewing him. It was TV gold.

I switched clubs for my last try and this one came up well short. I walked off the tee wondering what had just happened. None of my shots were closer than thirty feet to the hole and I knew right then that there would be no prize for me that day.

It made me mad and sad at the same time, but it was now over, and I would have to watch the winners get their prizes from Lobel. It was painful to watch, and I knew it was not my best effort.

The producer told us the final would be on TV the next Saturday. Now I had to tell my friends and family about how it went and what day and time the final would be on. They all wanted to see it. At least there would be some comedy when it came to seeing how it went for me.

It was not the most enjoyable golf day I ever had, but that is the way golf goes. You never know what game you will have on any given day. On this day, I clearly did not have my best swing. It was an awesome experience though, and Erik got more camera time than most of the winners.

The story does have a happy conclusion. Lucky for me I was going to Chicago that night for the special work project. After arriving in Chicago, having a couple of beers, and telling my two work friends the story, I had no time to sulk that week due to the new project and skill I needed to learn.

The work project was a huge success, and it was the greatest break of my working life to be part of it. I was eventually able to move over to the marketing side of the insurance business and this led to great opportunities in both work and in golf.

In my golf collection lies the VCR tape of Beat the Pro. Writing this made me dig it out and watch it one more time. With the help of my friend Roy Eaton, who just happened to have a working VCR in his basement, we all got a chance to see it. It was still painful to watch the ending, but I was happy to share the memory and some laughs with my family and friends.

In the end, it was a tremendous experience and I learned about dealing with pressure and unrealistic expectations. Plus, I got to meet one of Boston's greatest all-time sports personalities, Bob Lobel! Overall, an amazing memory and experience.

Hole #3

WHEN LOSING IS WINNING AT THE COUNTRY CLUB

One of the tremendous benefits of the job I had was most of my clients belonged to top level golf courses and would invite me to play them. Early in my marketing career I was invited by one of my clients to play golf at the Eastward Ho! Golf Club in Chatham, MA. I should have known it was going to be a different kind of day when I saw my host and his son arrive by boat.

Although I knew Eastward Ho! was a fine private golf course, at this point in my golfing life (1991), I am not sure I fully appreciated the magnitude of the invite. In the past few years, this course has shot up the Top 100 rankings and is a "hot" place to play. We learned that firsthand two summers ago when we were invited by my wife Tina's work friends to play it, and British Open Champion Darren Clarke was playing two groups behind us.

Pro golfer and Rhode Island native Brad Faxon is an advocate for the quality of the course and has frequently mentioned his affinity for Eastward Ho! in interviews when he is asked about his favorite places to play. No doubt he is right, given the spectacular scenery, especially on the front nine. I certainly believe Faxon's hearty endorsement has helped with the Eastward Ho! rise in popularity on Top 100 golf course lists.

The weather was perfect the day we played with light wind. The pace of play was quick. I learned right away that my host believed in the axiom "no matter how you play, play fast." The course was not busy, and we scooted around in well under four hours. Hard not to enjoy a course like this and even though I was nervous, I played well, although like most rounds there were a few shots I would have liked to have back.

After the round we had a quick beer overlooking Pleasant Bay. My host apologized about the quick beer. He explained that his family had dinner plans that night. Before we parted ways, he asked me if I would mind being put on his short list of people he called if he had a last-minute cancellation to golf events he hosted.

Turns out, he and a couple of his salespeople were members at some of the top clubs around metro Boston. They entertained clients frequently during the golf season at these courses. He told me sometimes people backed out of the events at the last minute, and they needed an emergency replacement to complete the group.

I quickly agreed to his request to be on the list, and then my hosts headed back to their boat for the short trip across the bay. I headed to my car for the ride home and thoughts of where this could lead.

Fast forward 9 months. I received an urgent message to call my friend from Eastward Ho! A good amount of time had passed, and in my job, urgent calls meant there was some huge problem that needed to be solved yesterday. Funny thinking about it now in the days of cell phones and voicemail as the message was left with our department secretary who was determined to track me down.

When I returned the call, I was sure there was a major issue. I spoke to my client's assistant and the feeling worsened when she told me she had specific orders to find him and interrupt any meeting that he may have been in as we needed to talk as soon as possible.

There was no hello when my client answered the phone, only the question "what are you doing tomorrow?" Having long ago forgot the conversation about being a last-minute replacement for golf, I said wisely, "working, of course!"

His reply stunned me. He said emphatically "change your plans then, we need a fourth at The Country Club in Brookline, MA for a 1 pm tee time. Can you make it work?" Without thinking or even checking my schedule book, I replied quickly "of course I can." Before hanging up he asked for my handicap (thankfully I had one) and told me that his salesperson who we would be guests of was a bit of a stickler for the rules. He warned me that we would be playing a match against the member and his other guest, and the stakes would not be high, but the match would be highly competitive.

When I hung up, I was excited but left wondering what I had gotten myself into.

This invite happened before the days of GPS, so I left myself plenty of time to find my way to the course. It took me an extra pass before I made the correct turn on to Clyde Street, saw the driveway, and guard house for The Country Club.

My first surprise of the day happened when I approached the guard house. As I drove up and slowed down there appeared to be a man inside. This is something one would expect at the top-rated course in Massachusetts. I slowed down and rolled my window open and then realized it was a cardboard cutout with a police hat and uniform on!

I slid on past the cutout and the guard house, luckily not driving off the road as I peered around at the green fairways and famous large yellow clubhouse by the 18th green. That same 18th green that Curtis Strange got up and down from the front bunker to force a playoff with Nick Faldo at the 1988 US Open. Strange won the first of his two consecutive US Opens that Monday in an eighteen-hole playoff. If you are ever in the Fours in Quincy, MA, there is an iconic picture in the lobby of Strange in the bunker hitting the shot that got him into the playoff.

This would be a day of many firsts for me. After meeting our host and having him size me up while we hit balls on the range, we were approached by a group of men who would be our caddies for the day. It showed my lack of sophistication because I had never had a caddie before. The putting green is close to the first tee, and I hit a few nervous putts under my caddie's watchful eye.

It was go time, and it was a relief to get that first drive out of the way, and I hit one that was acceptable. Walking down that first fairway, I quickly adjusted to not having to carry my bag. What a nice sensation of freedom it was to just walk and talk with the others in the group while the caddies followed close behind.

The first hole at TCC is no easy starting hole. It played well over four hundred yards and was a gentle dog leg left. My drive was on the right side of the fairway, and I had a long iron into the green. I was wide right with my approach shot and had a tough little flop shot over a bunker to get the ball safely on the green. I hit a soft high shot that spun to a stop about seven feet from the hole.

Not being used to having a caddie, I marked my ball and put it in my pocket. My caddie came over and gave me a nudge and asked for the ball. He wanted to make sure it was clean before I rolled it. What a joy this caddie thing was!

When I re-marked the ball, my caddie was right behind me, and he had already read the putt. The putt looked to my uneducated eye to be a tiny bit outside the left edge of the hole. I was shocked when his instruction to me in no uncertain terms was "right edge, firm." He left no doubt, and he also left no doubt that our team needed the putt to tie the hole.

First crisis of the day for me. Believe myself or believe the caddie. I made a quick decision that he must know these greens better than I do, and I should listen to him. I rolled it nicely on the quicker than I was accustomed to greens, and it fell just inside the right edge for a nice up and down par to start the round.

Brimming with confidence with my new friend for the day, I headed to the second tee much more relaxed than I was on the first tee.

Things were going well with our new partnership until we reached the 4th hole. The 4th was a short hole and I hit less than driver off the tee and laid up at the top of a hill. It looked to me that I would be left with a one hundred yard shot downhill. Perfect for my sand wedge, or at least that is what I thought.

By this time, my caddie had seen me hit a few shots, but to my surprise he pulled my pitching wedge from the bag. When I objected, he told me the sand wedge was not enough club and the pitching wedge was perfect. So far, he had been correct on all his advice, and I figured why not trust him again?

The shot was a thing of beauty and flew high and true, right over the back of the green and down into the woods. I handed the club back to him and all the goodwill from the first three holes evaporated quickly.

We found the ball and after I chunked it out of the woods to get the ball back in play, I made an angry double bogey six. I can see the shot clearly even to this day, and it still makes me angry. Guess it may be time to let it go.

The round went on and there were the usual highs and lows that every round of golf seems to bring. Some pars, one birdie, and unfortunately a couple of "others." The weather was a bit cold and chilly for a New England May day, but our match was a close one with the front nine being halved (tied).

For the record, this was not a big money match, a two-dollar Nassau (standard golf bet that is three bets, one bet on the front nine, one bet on the back nine and the last for the overall 18-hole match). It was a highly competitive match and even the caddies seemed into it. Come to find out later, they had some side money bet on the match. Good thing I did not know this when playing as I was nervous enough already.

When we arrived at the famous 17th hole our side was one up. The 17th hole has great history as it was the site of Justin Leonard's monster putt to help the USA win the Ryder Cup in 1999. It was the site too of Harry Vardon's bogey to Francis Ouimet's birdie to help Ouimet to his great upset playoff victory in the US Open in 1913.

This day the pin was on the back level of the green and my ball was on the front. A weak putt by me up the hill well short of the hole led to a costly bogey for our team and made the match even. Our opponents briskly headed towards the 18th tee with all the momentum in the match, and I was walking a bit dejectedly behind them when my partner caught me and told me to slow down.

My partner's next words stunned me. He said, we have a choice here. If we win the match on 18, we win four dollars. My guy will be cordial, and we will go into the locker room bar, collect our money, and he will buy us one beer. After the one beer he will leave, and we will need to leave too.

My partner then said we have another choice. We can lose the 18th hole, give him the four dollars and we will sit, drink, and eat as long as we want, and you will have plenty of time to explore the locker room and see all the historic memorabilia it holds.

This was a first for me and certainly against my natural competitive instinct. Our opponents had the tee and hit good shots in play. My partner showed me what he thought we should do and hit a hook left out of bounds and then another one into some deep grass. He was going to be out of the hole for sure.

With my partner in trouble, I hit my tee shot a mile right and had a long iron to the green. My next shot was short and found the deep bunker in front of the 18th green. Things got worse when my bunker shot carried over the back of the green. I chipped on and with two putts made a six, one more shot than both our opponents made. Game, set, and match and a huge smile from our host as we walked towards the bar to settle the bets and enjoy at least one post round libation.

Just like my partner predicted, his guy was in a jovial mood and the drinks and appetizers flowed for two hours. We ate, drank, and were regaled with numerous golf stories from our host. We had plenty of time to wander around and see the many items of golf history inside the locker room. It was an unbelievable golf experience.

Did I tank the match? I would be lying if I said I wanted to play the 18th hole badly. When I was in the bunker all I could think about was what my partner had said on the walk to the 18th tee and how much more fun we would have if we lost. The thought of losing was planted in my head, and I delivered even though I really wanted to hit a good shot from the sand trap and finish well.

Do I regret losing the match? Not one bit; it was the best four dollars I have ever spent. In the end, this turned out to be the only time (so far) that I have played The Country Club. I have returned to see the 1999 Ryder Cup, 2013 US Amateur and the 2022 US Open. I have been invited two other times to play it, but sadly, the weather has not cooperated.

Even years later I can remember the excitement of the day and the fun we had during and after the round. It was an invite I am still grateful for and a round I will never forget. It was certainly one of the most unique golf experiences of my life.

One of the only times in my life when I lost but no doubt, really won!

Hole #4

PEBBLE BEACH AND BEGINNER'S LUCK?

It was 1996 and I worked for CNA Insurance, and our office was in Quincy, MA. Ironic, as our office was located on the former site of the famous Quincy Bargain Center. A Quincy landmark and iconic business where my grandmother Edith Bredesen worked in the men's underwear and sock department when I was in school. I always had good socks and underwear growing up, even if they smelled a little smokey when I first got them. The "Bargie," specialized in the sale of fire damaged merchandise.

So, you may say, what does The Bargain Center have to do with Pebble Beach? It is just a coincidence that I worked at the same location as my grandmother, and this is the place that started my Pebble Beach journey.

When I worked for CNA, the company was heavily invested in CAM Programs (CAM standing for Commercial Affiliated Markets). A brief explanation of CAM: CAM was a dividend producing group for homogeneous types of business that we wanted to insure.

CAM is important, because if not for it, I may not have ended up at Pebble Beach. My friend and work colleague Gladys Morales convinced me that it would be a prudent idea for the both of us to attend the Plastics Association of America convention in Boston.

This was one of our CAM program groups. Against my judgment, Gladys convinced me we should attend this convention and acquire a greater level of expertise on this group. My customers had not had success selling this program, and I thought going to the convention was a waste of time. Gladys reasoned with me that at the worst it was a chance to go into Boston and do something different for a day. After some thought I gave in and begrudgingly tagged along with her and one of our underwriters.

Sometimes, good things happen when you least expect it. A month after we attended this convention, I received a call from the Plastics Processers Association. The call relayed the exciting news to me that they had drawn my business card from the hundreds they collected at the convention in Boston, and I had won their raffle grand prize, round trip airline tickets anywhere in the country.

After a brief discussion, it was decided that to get maximum value for the airfare, a flight would be booked to San Francisco. The trip would include time to explore San Francisco and a stop, at to me what was the number one golf course in the USA, Pebble Beach. A dream golf course for me to play.

The building where I worked in Quincy had a retail section on the first floor. One of the stores was a Buck A Book. The store carried books that had not been sold by the big-name retailers and they would sell them for discounted prices. Once in a while I would find a real bargain, and one of my best finds was a coffee table book called *A Paradise called Pebble Beach by Ray A. March*.

This book gave the complete history of how Samuel Morse built the course at Pebble Beach with many pictures of how it was done. In addition, the book gave a detailed description and multiple pictures of each hole at Pebble. Today, this would not be so important, but this was 1996 and it was pre-Google, and before every golf course had information and pictures easily available on the web.

I read that book more diligently than any book I had read in high school, and I knew the holes inside and out. I studied each hole over and over from the pictures in the book. To think that I would actually go there, and play it was a dream that I never thought would come true. But with a little luck, this dream would come true soon.

After phone calls to Pebble Beach to make sure the dates worked, the trip was planned for September 1996. We would fly to San Francisco, rent a car, and make the drive to Pebble. To ensure I could play, we had made a reservation at the Inn at Spanish Bay. According to the pleasant reservation agent, staying at a Pebble Beach property would be the only way a single player could get a tee time on Pebble Beach.

This trip was before the days of GPS, and it was always an adventure going to Logan Airport in Boston. The morning of the trip was no exception and there had been a major accident on the Southeast Expressway. Time was ticking away, and it looked like this long-planned trip was going to crash due to Boston traffic.

Somehow, we got to curbside check-in and dropped off the bags and managed to check in a half hour before the flight was to leave. Security was light in those days, and I parked the car and ran back to the terminal, and we made it to the gate, minutes before the flight finished boarding.

Things went smoothly after this, and we made our way from San Francisco to the Inn at Spanish Bay in time to have a drink and wait for the bagpiper to appear out of the sand dunes. The bagpiper appears each night at dusk, and you can hear the unmistakable sounds of the bagpipes floating out over the dunes. It sounded hauntingly beautiful and certainly built my anticipation for the round of golf the next day.

There was a message from the pro shop at check in letting me know my tee time would be 11:20 am the next day. This was exciting news, and I was happy to know the tee time and was thankful it was not early in the morning.

I was nervous but excited when I arrived at the course the next morning. In my research for the trip, I had neglected to notice that the driving range was away from the clubhouse. It was going to be impossible for me to have time to get to the range and warm up. This would be no problem, given the majority of my rounds were played on public courses with no practice ranges. The putting green was close to the pro shop, so I headed there as the Pebble Beach greens were notoriously small and fast. Rolling some practice putts would be smart preparation for my round.

While on the putting green, I noticed commotion in the nearby pro shop. A group of three players had arrived and were renting clubs. I thought this was odd. In my mind I thought players who would be willing to pay the astronomical price to play one of the country's great golf courses, would all be highly skilled players. I could not imagine any skilled golfer wanting to play Pebble Beach without their own golf clubs.

As I observed the chaos going on with the rental three-some getting their clubs, the unnerving thought crossed my mind that this threesome could be my partners for the day. I dismissed this thought quickly thinking that this could not happen to me for my dream round of golf at Pebble Beach.

My tee time came and much to my horror, the group with the rental clubs approached the starter at the same time I did. It became clear that the unthinkable was going to happen. I had no doubt now I was going spend the most anticipated round of my golf life, with the rental club three-some.

We were introduced and the first two I met were hus-band and wife. The third was the person I met next, and she would be my cart partner for the round. My partner appeared nervous, certainly more nervous than I was. She then gave me the first hint of what I was in for by telling me she was not a very experienced golfer. Oh boy I thought, what happened to the low handicap players I thought I would be playing with?

We were on the tee, and nobody seemed ready to hit so I volunteered to lead off the group. The first tee at Pebble is a nerve-wracking place. There are groups of golfers and non-golfers always milling around the area. The opening tee shot is a tight one, with hotel buildings on both sides of the fairway that were in easy range of an errant drive.

I was glad to get this swing out of the way and my trusty Pebble Beach book said it might be good to hit less than driver off the first tee. I hit a drawing 3 wood that stopped just short of a large tree on the left side of the fairway.

It was the last shot I hit for 20 minutes.

My partners shots were sprayed all over the course. My male counterpart did what I feared doing and hit a slice to the right that bounced off the balcony of one of the hotel rooms with a loud clang. He reloaded and thankfully hit one that stayed in play.

Now it was the ladies turn. My cart partner was last, and the result was not pretty. Two whiffs, a ground ball, then another, then another. At this rate it was going to be a long time till I hit my second shot. I lost count but she may have hit ten shots to get to my ball. The course being cart path only did not help the situation either. Her friends were doing a little better, but I believe we would have set a record for shots hit on the first hole if such a record existed.

Finally, I did get to hit my second shot with a nine iron and came up short. I chipped on to the green and then waited a long time again for my turn. I was unsettled with all the waiting, and I missed my downhill par putt by a mile. I missed the comeback putt too for an ugly double bogey six to start. It was not the way I had visualized my start, but I was relieved the first hole was over. Watching my group play, it did make me wonder if we could finish this round in under seven hours.

As we approached the second tee, we were about to learn more about pace of play. The course marshal arrived the same time we arrived at the second tee, and I figured this was going to be interesting.

With an incredulous look the marshal asked us, "folks, what is going on here?" Without giving us time to answer he continued, "you are a hole and a half behind the group in front of you after only one hole. We have groups for three more hours going off the first tee and many of them will not finish their round if this keeps up. Please work to pick up the pace as fast as you can. If you do not, we will need to move you back to your correct position on the course." It was embarrassing to hear this reprimand, but it was desperately needed.

This was when my cart partner decided to come clean about her golf expertise.

She said she had not planned to play but her friends convinced her to come along. It turned out, her only golf experience had been to go to a driving range. She had never played a round on a real course! The convention she was attending was being held at The Inn at Spanish Bay, and her firm was paying for all the expenses from the trip including golf. I was stunned by this news, but we needed a plan since the pressure was now on us to move along faster.

My solution was simple. I proposed to my partner that we would both hit drives and then we would play from wherever the best shot ended up. My partner loved the idea but was unsure if the course would allow it. My response was for $350 they will let you do whatever you want so long as we keep up the pace.

She agreed to this idea quickly and this took the pressure off the group. In short order we were back in our correct place on the course. This made the marshal who had now been watching us happy, and he disappeared for the balance of the round.

When I tell this story, normally about this time someone will interrupt and comment about how angry I must have been about this situation.

At the time it was happening, I could not believe it and there was certainly some anger and resentment about the bad luck of drawing this group. Once we got caught up to the group in front of us the tension was gone, and I decided that I would not let this pairing ruin for me what was the most anticipated round of my golf life. I forced myself to walk more and take in all the sights of the spectacular scenery of the Monterey Peninsula. There was no rush since play was moving along at a slow but steady pace.

The round had highlights, a birdie at the famous and short par 3 seventh hole and a par at number eight. Jack Nicklaus says the eighth at Pebble is the best par four in the world and there is no doubt that the second shot over the canyon and water is one of the most unique and terrifying shots in golf. I was thrilled to have success on those two holes.

I had a nice run on the back, with pars at 10, 11 and 12 but my finish was not what I had hoped for.

When we headed to the 18th, I wanted to make par in the worst way as eighteen is one of the most famous finishing holes in golf. The Pacific Ocean and Stillwater Cove border the left side of the fairway with beautiful homes, and the clubhouse to the right. The perfect blending of nature and golf.

A good drive and layup on this par five and I have what I thought was an easy nine iron into the smallish green. This was the only time during the day after the first hole where my partners bothered me. They were talking and taking pictures and making noise while I was trying to hit my shot. It rattled my concentration and my shot ended up short, landing in the face of the bunker on the right front of the green and rolling back to the bottom of the bunker.

I blasted out of the bunker to ten feet, but my par putt slid by the hole. It was a disappointing bogey finish.

An eighty-three in my first attempt at Pebble was a respectable score, especially with all that was going on that day.

The five- and one-half hour odyssey of a round had finally ended. We shook hands, took a few more pictures and I exchanged business cards with my cart partner. Little did I know then that this would lead to one of the most interesting letters I have ever received.

Two weeks after returning from Pebble, a letter with a return address I did not recognize arrived at my home. I opened it and wondered what it could be about. It did not take me long to figure it out.

The letter was from my cart partner from that day at Pebble. When she returned home after her convention, she told her husband about her Pebble adventure. Her husband could not believe that she had allowed her friends to convince her to play golf and he insisted she write me a letter and apologize for ruining my day!

She wrote the letter, and it was a long letter explaining to me why she made the decision to play. She mentioned two times that she was sorry to "ruin" my day. She invited me to join her husband and her for a round of golf at their course. It was clear she felt badly about what happened and wanted to make things "right."

Her husband was supposed to have played in her spot in our group but was called away for a work emergency at the last minute. She told me he was disappointed to have missed his chance to play Pebble Beach but was just as disappointed with her decision to play that day.

I did write her back and let her know that she did not ruin my day. I told her I made the best of the day and was able to take in the scenery at Pebble Beach more than I might have in another round. I thanked her for the invite to play and hoped we would be able to do it someday in the future. Maybe it was for the best, but that round she invited me for never took place.

I might have felt differently if she and her friends had adversely affected my play, but except for the first and last hole they were not a factor. In the end, they were nice people, and I was thrilled that I got the chance to play one of the best golf courses in the world, Pebble Beach!

It is the kind of story that you could just not fathom happening and all these years later I still have her letter to remind me of what a day it was. It was certainly a day like no other I have ever had on a golf course!

Hole #5

HAVE CLUBS WILL TRAVEL

I was an accounting major in college. I quickly realized that being a CPA or working in public accounting was not going to be the route my career traveled. There were two reasons that made me come to this conclusion. Reason number one: I liked to ski in the winter, and the public accounting busy season during the prime ski months would make skiing impossible. Reason two: as I progressed through my accounting major curriculum, I came to realize that my average grades in my accounting classes were not going to cut it with the lofty standards the large accounting firms had for new recruits.

Sometimes things just work out the right way.

That is when the insurance industry came knocking on my door. Good thing I answered because it led to a forty plus year career.

To be honest, I was looking for any kind of accounting job coming out of college and one of the job advertisements I answered was for a premium auditor position. It was a job that required an accounting degree but was not a job that was on the path to be a CPA. Since entry level jobs were scarce in 1978, anything that looked like an accounting job was good enough for me.

That the job came with a company car, expense account and the ability to set your own schedule made it sound attractive. I applied and was hired!

After my training was complete, my "have clubs will travel" adventures began. The first trip was to Northern New England and New Hampshire.

My first premium audit appointments began with a trip to the North Conway area of New Hampshire. The person who covered the territory had left the company and there was a need for someone to work the area. It was summer and I had plenty of daylight after work. A perfect opportunity to bring my clubs and find golf courses to play.

I played some quality courses and a few real mountain goat tracks, but I really did not care because it was more enjoyable being out playing golf than sitting in my hotel room. I managed to do a couple of other adventurous endeavors on these trips, like taking a plane ride over the Presidential Range and Mt. Washington and another time taking a pontoon plane up for a spin and a couple touch and goes on Lake Winnipesaukee. The pilot even let me handle the controls for a short time while we circled the lake.

A change in jobs benefited me and opened up a whole new level of travel. When I started to work for CNA Insurance, they asked each premium auditor to travel every year and help out in other parts of the Eastern Region. These trips involved a week-long stay, working in a foreign territory. I spent time in New York, New Jersey, Connecticut, and Virginia.

By this time, I had learned much more about golf and golf travel and always did research into the nicer courses in each area. Through these trips I managed to squeeze in rounds at fine courses, including Richter Park in Danbury, CT (at that time a top one hundred course you could play) Shennecossett in Groton, CT and the first top tier course I had ever played, The Golden Horseshoe, in Williamsburg, VA.

I had never been to a place like The Golden Horseshoe. The clubhouse and hotel were both stately looking old southern style buildings in the downtown of historic Williamsburg, VA. The course looked to be in immaculate condition.

Due to my audit visit running long, I barely made the tee time and was changing my clothes in the car to try to make it to the course for my scheduled time. When I arrived and was running to the clubhouse to pay, the pro saw me and told me to slow down. He said the course was not busy at this time and to take my time and go warm up and relax. I took a deep breath and headed to the range to get ready.

The course meandered through the forest and there were herds of deer sauntering around the property. I was alone with nobody playing near me and the sounds of the woods were serene, a pleasant change from my hectic drive earlier. This course had the first island green I had ever played, and I was pleased when my shot managed to find the green.

When I finished, I still wanted to play more, so I jumped on and played their par three course after my round. It was an enjoyable way to finish an exciting day at an outstanding golf resort.

Being on the road and finding a place to play takes luck sometimes. A couple of years after playing the Golden

Horseshoe, I was sent to Long Island for a week to work. I had read a recent article in one of the golf publications about this golf complex called Bethpage State Park and the mystical course Bethpage Black.

The gist of the article was that the course was a masterpiece built by famed golf course architect A.W. Tillinghast but had fallen into a bit of disrepair. The course was still quite popular to play and was considered a great challenge. Since my hotel was about five miles from the Bethpage complex, I decided to take a ride over one afternoon during my stay and check it out.

The parking lot was jammed on this warm weekday afternoon, and I luckily found a parking space near the clubhouse. When I enquired about playing, the cashier replied, "there is a threesome heading to the first tee of the Black Course, if you can be ready to go in five minutes, you can head out with them if you pay now." As I raced away, he yelled a warning that there was only a little more than five hours daylight left and your group may not finish all eighteen holes. At this point it was too late to back out of the round and I was going to have to hustle to get back to my car and then over to the first tee.

Not being shy, I changed my clothes right next to the car and grabbed my clubs and sprinted to the tee. I surveyed the scene and I saw the famous sign warning golfers that the Black Course was for expert players only. It was the golf equivalent of a black diamond ski slope. It was too late to turn back, so I hustled on to the first tee and introduced myself to my group. All were locals, two friends and another single like me. I was worried about the sign and wondered if my partners were experts. It turned out, they were just like me and wanted to give the Black Course a try.

The course was long and hard, and play was slow. My most memorable shot was an up and down from the left side of the second hole. After a solid par at the first hole, I hit two poor shots to the left on number two, the side on which you could not miss. With a steep incline staring me in the face, I hit a nice flop shot that rolled out to about a foot and an unlikely par.

By the time we arrived on the 17th tee, the sun had set, and we were playing in fading twilight. We all hit shots and somehow found them on or around the green.

The 18th hole was another story, as now it was dark. We tried to play it, but we needed glow balls to be able to find where our drives ended up. After two balls were lost, we decided to hit short pitch shots up the hill to the green. We found all the balls and putted out. I was glad to find a place to eat and head back to my hotel given that the Black Course is one of the hardest walks in golf. It was well worth it to get the chance to experience it. A few years after I played the Black Course the USGA came in and completely revamped the course, and it has held numerous major championships since then.

My then job with CNA gave me the chance to travel to Chicago for business. I had read about the Cog Hill golf complex just outside the city that was one of the top public golf facilities in the country. The PGA Tour in those days stopped at this site and played the Dubsdread Course. Not all my road trips went smoothly and this one sits at the top of the list for screw ups.

My plan was to fly in a day early and rent a car for the day to get over to Cog Hill. All was going well until I decided to lighten my wallet of unnecessary items before the trip. When I arrived at the car rental counter, a small issue arose. To rent a car you needed to show a license, and mine was now at home with my other "unnecessary" items. In the post 9/11 days this could never happen, but I was able to get on the airplane without my license. I begged the rental agent to still rent me a car but there was no way she could do it. I asked the counter staff if any of them knew a golf course close to O'Hare Airport. Someone at the desk thought the closest was a place called White Pine Golf Course.

I headed to the taxi stand in hopes that it was not a long ride.

My cab driver was not a golfer and did not know the area. I gave him the name and address, but we just seemed to go around in circles. We were having language issues too, and I could see the fare piling up and begged him to pull into a gas station. I bought a map and found the course on it. Thankfully, it was close, and I was happy to arrive.

The adventure continued when I checked in at the course. I had decided to use rental clubs (Cog Hill had nice clubs for rentals, but not this place) and I could not hit the driver in my set of clubs. I hit the three iron from the rental set off the tee all day but given all that happened I was glad I got to play. Even if it was with a set of poor-quality clubs.

My last issue to overcome was I needed to find a way into the city and to my hotel downtown. Thankfully, there was a train station close to White Pine and one of the course employees gave me a ride over to the station. After the morning cab experience, I wanted nothing to do with another cab ride fiasco.

I returned to Chicago a year later and this time remembered my license. I was able to play both Cog Hill and the Sidney Marovitz Golf Course which is right in the city on the shores of Lake Michigan. When we had to bring our luggage into the last day of the sales seminar, I was the only one dragging along golf clubs. I got odd looks from the non-golfers in the class, but the instructor was a golfer and got a kick out of someone taking advantage of the trip to play golf.

At CNA, our department always had an annual training meeting. I was able to play courses around our office in Reading, PA along with trips to Shawnee on the Delaware (home to a PGA Tour event at one time) and The Skytop Lodge.

I loved Skytop because the golf course wound around the old-style hotel, and we could walk on and play any morning before our meeting. This worked until one morning when the temperature dipped below freezing and frost set in. We played anyway and after four holes the greens keeper approached us and asked us if we had noticed the footprints we were leaving. We said no and he replied that it would be prudent if we left the course because it was closed, and we were causing damage to the grass. Luckily, we did not get in trouble with our management team for this mistake.

Times change and so did my job. I was fortunate to be hired by Peerless Insurance which had been purchased by Liberty Mutual Insurance in 1999. My time at Peerless expanded my business career and golf travel options.

The Peerless home office was located in Keene, NH. Keene has an outstanding 36-hole public golf facility called Bretwood Golf Course. It is a hidden gem, and I would try to scoot over to play one of the two 18-hole courses any time I had extra time while in Keene. Keene Country Club was the private course in town, and I enjoyed playing there at events we hosted for clients.

Our management team at Liberty decided to start having sales meetings for us in different regions of the country each year. This offered great opportunities to explore and play golf in multiple states that I might not have otherwise visited.

The first meeting was in Charleston, SC and my now wife Tina came along with me. With help from her brother and PGA Pro Ted O'Rourke, we were able to play the beautiful Yeamans Hall Club. Designed by Seth Raynor, it is now a perennial top one hundred course in the country. We just beat a monsoon rainstorm to finish, and Tina will never forget the voracious mosquitoes that tried to eat her alive!

The playing of top one hundred courses continued when the meeting was held in Hollywood, CA. Tina joined me again, and we trekked south to San Diego and visited with Tina's friend Deb Finnegan. Deb, being a San Diego resident, was able to get us a tee time on the US Open South Course at Torrey Pines. Deb and Tina were real champions in this round, as they were incorrectly directed to play from the men's white tees, making the course quite long for them. It was a banner day for me at Torrey with three birdies including one on the par 5 18th hole. It was an exciting way to finish the round!

We celebrated this round with a great dinner and sunset at the Torrey Pines Lodge with Deb and her husband John. A perfect way to end a California day.

Speaking of US Open courses, the sales meeting was held one year in Seattle, and I headed out early to play Chambers Bay. This course was so fun to play, and I played with three locals who explained to me that they were still angry with what the USGA did to the course and how badly they made it look on TV for the 2015 US Open. I loved Chambers Bay, and it would rank at the top of my all-time underrated courses played. You can see the sparkling waters of Puget Sound from nearly every hole and the course reminded me of the links courses of Ireland and Scotland.

These local guys taught me a good lesson about playing golf in the Pacific Northwest. When the icy rain came down in buckets on the 3rd and 4th holes, I asked my partners when they thought we would be heading to the clubhouse. Their answer was "we never quit dude; do you know where you are? This is the Pacific Northwest, and it rains here all the time!" We played on and were rewarded with brilliant sunshine and a cloudless sky for the last four holes.

Our finest US Open experience was at the renowned Pebble Beach Golf Resort. I was sent there for a work incentive trip, and there was no way Tina was staying home. Even though my manager told us no guests were allowed, we decided to gamble, and Tina flew to Pebble Beach the day after me. Given the cost of staying at Pebble, this may have been our only chance to do this trip for a reasonable price.

Tina was not going to attend any of the company events, and she was happy to be on her own and enjoy the beautiful resort. When Tina arrived at our suite at the Inn at Spanish Bay and saw the view and luxurious accommodations, she told me she was not leaving the room for the entire stay!

In the end, I managed not to get fired for disobeying my manager and we had a great couple of days staying at the beautiful Inn at Spanish Bay, exploring the Monterrey Peninsula, and playing Pebble Beach together.

Not all of the sales meetings were near US Open sites, but I managed to play some memorable courses in Denver, San Antonio, and Miami. The courses I played were all public and all quite different from the courses here in the Northeast. I certainly loved playing in the thin air in Denver with the ball going farther.

My last and favorite golf adventure goes back to my CNA days. My territory was the entire state of Massachusetts and I needed to make a trip out to North Adams to visit a client who wanted to increase their business with our company. You could not find a place to travel to in the state much farther from my home in Sandwich than to North Adams.

I had good friends from college who would always talk about the best course in Massachusetts that nobody knew about. That course was Taconic, on the campus of Williams College. I looked at the map and saw an opportunity to find out what all the talk was about, so I booked an overnight trip out to North Adams.

The meeting went well and did not last as long as I expected. At the end of the meeting, one of the agency owners asked me what my plans were for the night seeing I was a long way from home. It was the perfect question at the perfect time.

I told my client I had my golf clubs in my trunk and planned to stop over at Taconic to see if I could play. He gave me a quizzical look and asked if I had plans to meet a member to play. I replied that I did not know a member and was hoping to walk on. My client told me that I might not get on and if I did it would be an expensive round playing without a member. He smiled and said he was a member and had a plan.

He made three phone calls and next thing I knew I was following him over to Taconic. My new friend had made arrangements to have the family au pair meet him at the course with some golf clothes. He had spoken to the starter at the course too, and it was not busy at all so we would be able to play, and our round should be a speedy one.

Turns out, it was the Monday after the club held one of their major three-day tournaments. Many members participated and most had played their share of golf over the past few days. My client had played in it too but was kind enough to take me out to play the course even though he was tired from the weekend event.

You do meet the most generous people through golf!

We grabbed a cart and sped around the course. Past the large white house that the Shah of Iran's son stayed in when he attended Williams and by the spot where Jack Nicklaus made a hole-in-one in the 1956 US Junior Amateur.

Every hole was different and memorable but my favorite on the course was the 18th hole. You hit your drive back towards the old-style clubhouse and outdoor veranda that is right behind the 18th green. It is a shorter par five, and long hitters can reach the green in two. We both got close to the green in two and both made birdies. A wonderful way to close out a round that only took two and a half hours to play!

Since my partner had a young family and was pushing things at home a little by playing after the weekend event, there was a quick beer and then he was off. Sadly, it was the last time I visited out that way for work, but I could not be more thankful for the outstanding golf experience I had.

These experiences reinforced what I already knew: that business travel and golf mix well and it always pays to have your clubs ready to roll. I feel fortunate to have been able to play the courses mentioned here and many more due to business travel.

Hole #6

ADVENTURE AT THE OLD COURSE

It was July of 2000, and The Open championship was being held at the Home of Golf, St Andrews, Scotland. Tiger Woods is lapping the field to win going away. A few thousand miles away in Ogunquit, ME my father is watching the romp on his jumbo TV in his living room. Being recently retired, in good health, and ready to travel a little, my dad had an idea that it would be a good time for my brother Mark and me to join him to visit Scotland and play St Andrews. Since my brother and I both had younger children, there was some convincing to do, but a week or so later the arrangements were in place for our trip in the beginning of October.

Getting a tee time on the Old Course is never easy and playing it in an Open year is normally even harder. We were late in making our arrangements, and there were no tee times available on the Old Course for our travel dates. A unique feature of the Old Course is it is a public golf course, and every day there are tee times set aside for public play. A lottery is held daily (except for Sunday when the Old Course becomes a public park) called the Ballot. The Ballot is drawn 48 hours prior to the day of play, and our tour company would manage the details of entering us in the Ballot each day.

When we departed from Logan International Airport in Boston, we were looking forward to playing an excellent group of Scottish courses in Gullane and North Berwick along with St Andrews New, Jubilee and Kingsbarn. We were hoping for good luck with landing a time on the Old Course too.

When we arrived in a drizzle at Glasgow Airport, we were met by our cheery local rep from our tour company. His first words after greeting us were, "I have good news and bad news for you gentlemen."

We said lead with the good news, and the good news was while we were flying, he had received a cancellation for the Old Course during our week's stay. What could be the bad news I thought. Quickly while I was still stuck on that thought, he told us that the tee time was for two, not three players. A slight problem since we had a threesome.

Since my dad was paying for the trip and my brother had a sore back, I told them they should take the tee time and I would find another way to play the Old Course. I had done extensive research on the Old Course prior to the trip and knew there was always a chance to "walk on" and get a tee time on any given day.

From my research about playing the Old Course I had learned if you were willing to get up early, there was a line that formed every day for "walk on players." With international travel snafus, St. Andrews University students sometime partying too much the night before and a host of other reasons, there were always spots open for play every day on the Old Course.

With that we headed off to Gullane and Berwick for a couple of perfect weather days and golf before heading to the Home of Golf.

I will never forget the ride into St Andrews. After driving through small older villages after we exited the M90 highway, the course appeared quickly, like a surprise. It was so green, and I remember thinking I have actually made it to the Home of Golf. This was unbelievable!

We warmed up with rounds on Kingsbarns (one of my favorite courses) and the Jubilee course at St Andrews. These rounds were played in a real howling North Sea gale. It was a first for all of us playing in wind like this and we found it really wore us down.

The day arrived for the Old, and my plan was set. My Dad and brother had an early afternoon tee time on the Old Course, and I would be rising at 4 am and make the short walk from Rusacks Hotel to the gathering spot by the first tee at the Old Course for "walk on players."

I was not sure what to expect at 4:15 am but when I arrived, I was cheerfully greeted by a brave small band of golfers. They informed me that the line was an honor system, and I was number eight in line that morning. They let me know that I would keep this number till the starter showed up right on the dot at 7 am.

As I started talking to people around me, I learned that numbers 1 and 2 in line arrived at midnight after dinner and multiple cocktails with their wives. With the boldness of alcohol and the permission of their significant others, they headed straight to the tee when dinner and drinks were done. It was a total whim and not planned on their vacation itinerary. Neither had clubs but they were in St

Andrews, both avid golfers, and thought this may be their only chance ever to play the Old. Their plan was to rent clubs first thing in the morning.

The others in line were from all over the globe. A couple from California, a group of four friends from the Midwest and a couple of Aussies and Swedes. There was also an assistant golf pro from Maryland and an American working on an oil rig in the North Sea. All sharing the same dream to somehow find a way on to the Old Course.

The night was cold, but the conversations were friendly and warm. No pushing and shoving, just stories about where they came from, the clubs they played at, and how they ended up at this place. A camaraderie of strangers with the hope for the golfing experience of a lifetime.

At 6:00 am Sheena and Jack Willoughby, the former owners of The Dunvegan (a great pub and hotel a nine iron from the first tee) arrived with hot coffee for the group. It was much appreciated since the temperature was in the low 40s and we all needed a little warmth. They came because a number of people in line that morning were staying at their hotel.

Right on cue, our starter for the day arrived punctually at 7am. He gathered the group of now twenty-four together for his daily speech.

He said if you are numbers 1-12 you should stay close by the tee. He advised us that there were openings this day and you just never know how many more spots could open up. The first tee time was 8 am and we now had 45 minutes. He told us we had time for a quick bite, but we should try to be in the first tee area around 8 am just in case there were no shows early.

This was great news for me since I was hungry and cold, and nothing sounded better at this point than my fifth full Scottish Breakfast of the week from the picture window at Rusacks Hotel. From here, I could see all that was going on with the first tee at the Old Course. For a golfer, this is the best breakfast spot in the world. From a seat near the large picture window, you could watch over and over people living out their life's dream of playing the Old Course as they hit their first tee shot and walked down the first fairway.

My breakfast arrived just before 8am. When my Full Scottish arrived, I glanced out the picture window to see the foursome of people at 3,4,5 and 6 in line from last night on the tee getting loose and ready to lead off the day. At this point I had no idea what had happened to the guys at 1 and 2 but now I was close to being on the tee. I scoffed down the breakfast and ran across the first and eighteenth fairways to see what was going on.

As mentioned before, the guys who were 1 and 2 needed to rent golf clubs. In an odd situation, the rental shop did not open till 8:30. Since they had no clubs yet, 1 and 2 had to pass on the first tee time. The four friends behind them in line got out together. It was highly unusual for a foursome of people in line together to get to play together we were told by the starter. These people had exceptionally good luck that day!

It gets a bit stranger. The guys who are 1 and 2 come back a little early and have their rental clubs. The 8:40 tee time is up soon, and the starter comes out to warn all of us about what he anticipates is going to take place.

Two local college students have the 8:40 tee time, and they are signed up to play as a twosome. The starter tells the guys who are 1 and 2 that you are up, and you can ask these two if you can join their twosome. The local custom is you must ask the group who has the tee time for permission to join them.

The starter warns all of us that these guys are wankers (British Isle slang for jerks), and they will say no to their request. He told us they do it all the time and it is their right, and he further quipped that most local town residents would never do this.

As the starter predicted, the two college boys smiled, shook their heads, and uttered a quick "no thank you" when 1 and 2 approached and asked to join them. The no was delivered in a demeaning tone (they clearly enjoyed doing it), and 1 and 2 were so mad they wanted to fight the two college boys. No fight broke out but there were many angry stares when these two strolled down number one from the now thirty-five people in line. Everyone in line now knew that two less people would play the Old Course that day due to the college students' decision. (That day the line grew to forty people and twenty-six got out).

Things moved quickly now, and the starter calls numbers 1,2,7 and 8. 8 is me! Wow, this is going to happen I thought to myself. There was another no-show group, and we would be on the tee shortly.

Like most events this day, things did not go as planned. When we were all called to pay our greens fee, the starter looked at the guy who was number 7 and said to him, "you have jeans on, you cannot play the Old Course in jeans." He told him to head to one of the golf shops and buy rain pants to cover the jeans and called number 9 to the tee.

Do not feel bad for 7, he got out two groups later. I ran into him after the round. It just cost him an extra fifty pounds to get the right pants.

No doubt I remember that first tee shot more than any other I have hit. There were all my new friends from the line, my now playing partners who I barely knew, and a smattering of tourists who had wandered over to watch the action. A low hooked drive left that ran a mile but stayed in bounds, another low hooked six iron that landed about thirty yards left of the first green, and then a chip to about a foot for an easy par. Well, not that easy!

It was a round like most, with good shots and a couple of bad ones. A string of four pars at the beginning of the round and hitting a five wood over the Hell Bunker on the par 5 fourteenth and making par were the highlights. On the lowlight side, a bad three putt on the famous 17th Road Hole (one of the toughest par fours in golf) after two good shots to the green and having an uphill birdie putt. I have never been so mad about a three putt!

There is no more enjoyable walk in golf than the walk up eighteen at the Old. Not the hardest hole ever but ending the journey of playing the Old is a wonderful way to finish. Often times, it is with a gallery of tourists and fellow golfers watching and applauding good shots from just behind the eighteenth green. It is quite memorable.

In another interesting Scottish rule, the wife of the number 2 guy in line decided to come watch and was allowed to walk with us for all eighteen holes. No charge for this!

It was nice to have her along because she took great pictures for me. My favorite one is me hitting my drive on eighteen with the majestic Royal & Ancient Clubhouse in the background. Aim at the clock was the advice I had read, and the picture shows I got that part right!

After I finished playing that day, I watched my dad and brother tee off on the Old. I took pictures of both with the same R&A clock I aimed at off the 18th tee, in the background to mark the time of their first shots.

After watching my brother and Dad tee off, I headed over to the New Course. We still had a tee time there and I did not want to waste it. I was paired with a family with a father who was eighty-two and his two adult children. They had come to St Andrews to try to play the Old but did not have success in the Ballot for the days they were in town.

The son told me that it was a lifetime family dream to play the Old Course and he had even tried to bribe the starter for a tee time. The starter told him that someone tries this tactic almost every day and he could not do it no matter how compelling the circumstances were. He also told the son he would lose his job if he were caught taking the bribe. Certainly, interesting to hear how often people try to do this.

After trying the Ballot for a couple of days, they had to "settle" for the New Course. Not a bad alternative, because the New Course is old and was opened for play in 1895 and is located on adjacent land to the Old Course. We all walked, and the 82-year-old dad played every hole but seventeen. He wanted to finish well and play the 18th hole, so he rested on seventeen so he could finish and play out eighteen. It was inspiring to play with this group and see my new 82-year-old friend stride proudly up the 18th hole!

By playing the New, I did miss one of the best moments of the trip.

My Dad and brother were finishing their round on the 18th of the Old and a large crowd had gathered around the green. My dad hit his approach shot onto the green, but the pin was on the far left and his shot had ended up on the far-right side of this large green. The caddie gave him a line and told him the putt had a sweeping right to left break to it and advised him to give it a hard rap. It was like the ball had a magnet in it according to my brother, and after a long voyage across the green it popped off the flagstick and into the hole for a birdie! The crowd broke out into applause, and this was certainly a fitting way for the trip to end for my dad!

This was one of my favorite golf days ever at the magical town of St Andrews. The best golf town in the world!

Hole #7

FREE FALLING

Falling from ladders has become a habit in my family. My brother Mark, my father Phil and I all fell off one. We are reminded all the time by family to stay off ladders, but once in a while I still find the need to climb one.

I am not sure why we all have fallen. As a kid, I had no fear of heights. Growing up in a neighborhood with trees, my friends and I would always be climbing them, especially the four trees at the top of Bayfield Road in Quincy, MA where I grew up. Sometimes we would sit up in the trees for hours and just talk. It was a safe place and I never remember anyone getting hurt or falling out of a tree. We must have been good climbers.

In the summer when my family would travel to Ogunquit, ME for vacation, tree climbing was a frequent activity to occupy my time. I loved to climb trees next to the house so I could look across at my parents and grandparents sitting at the dining room table. I never fell and was not afraid even though sometimes I would be up fifty feet in the air.

Seems like tree climbing is a lost art and I never see kids climb trees anymore. I am fairly sure neither of my sons ever climbed a tree. Kind of a sad thing, because it taught me how to be careful and make sure every step was secure.

Maybe not being afraid of heights is why my father thought my brother and I should start a painting business when we were in high school. We had no fear of climbing ladders and it seemed we could make good money doing it.

I learned to respect heights more in those days. No more so than on a day we were painting trim on a house that had us up twenty feet. While we were climbing to put our staging up on our ladders, one of the rungs on the wooden ladder broke while we were climbing, and I slipped down one rung. Somehow, the ladder held me. It was scary and after that we bought more secure staging that did not rely on ladders to support us. It may have been a lifesaver.

We had a couple minor issues with this new pump up staging but it was much better than the ladders and only once do I remember us getting the boards too far apart. This caused the board to slip off the staging but luckily, we were only a few feet off the ground and both able to jump off without any injury. The biggest casualty from this was the loss of a gallon of latex paint. It spilled and we had to work hard to clean it up so our customer would not know we made a mess of their yard.

Jumping ahead a number of years and now I am building my own house. With the help of Maine Post and Beam and my family and a few friends we set out to build a post and beam home in Sandwich, MA. I certainly learned much from the experience and did the interior and exterior painting and staining myself. By 1998 it was time for the exterior of the house to be stained again. I decided that I would do it myself. A fateful decision.

The house had a high peak on the driveway side and was a long climb up to reach it. The house also needed scraping and sanding due to the stain on the house peeling. It was a long and slow process and Fall and Winter were coming.

At this point in my life, I was more interested in golf than I was in painting and staining. I had taken time off to finish the job, but the weather was good and most afternoons I would head off to play at least a few holes of golf. This certainly dragged out the project longer than it should have gone.

Time flies and all of a sudden it was mid-November, and the house was not looking so hot. I needed to speed up and clamp down and get the job finished. Being November though, it was getting cold and on top of that, it was football season. What is better than a fall day and watching football late on a Sunday afternoon?

This Sunday, there was a 4 p.m. game I wanted to see. Boston favorite Doug Flutie was playing quarterback for the Buffalo Bills, and they were featured in the late afternoon time slot. It was chilly and I had been staining the house all day. I had one more small section to get to and I would be done. The only way I could get to this area was to put a step ladder up on the sub roof above the garage. I had done it before and did not think that there was risk in doing it again. Plus, it was getting dark, and I needed to move quickly.

It was now just before kickoff, and I hustled up onto the sub roof and took a plastic drop cloth up so any stain I spilled would not show up on the dark shingles of the sub roof. I quickly threw down the drop cloth and put the step ladder up so I could reach the one spot I needed to finish and get inside for the game. I had not paid much attention to how I had put the drop cloth down and the ladder, which was leaning on the house, was on the plastic drop cloth. I was moving fast and only thinking about finishing quickly.

This was a critical mistake.

When I started to climb and reached the spot needing stain, the ladder began to slip and, in an instant, I had fallen off of it and was rolling on the sub roof. Stain spilled all over the sub roof and there was nothing I could do to stop the fall. I rolled two or three times on the sub roof and before I could blink, I landed with a thud on the asphalt driveway. It was a seven-foot drop and I came down hard on my right wrist and elbow.

There was nobody home and I did not see anyone around in the neighborhood. I was dazed and when I tried to move my right arm, it did not cooperate. Stain had spilled all over the driveway now, and I started to wash it away with the garden hose. I even found a way to climb back on the sub roof and clean it up the best I could.

Luckily, my neighbor across the street had been home and noticed what was going on from his living room window. He came over to check on me and at this point I think the realization of what had taken place was setting in. I was dizzy and needed to sit down. My neighbor could see there was clearly something wrong and told me he thought it best to call an ambulance and get me to the emergency room. I was feeling weak and at this point knew there was something majorly wrong with my arm.

Next thing I knew, I was in the back of the ambulance heading for the emergency room at Falmouth Hospital. My elbow and arm were now throbbing, and I knew for sure something was broken. Even then I realized it could have been much worse and certainly I could have landed on my head or neck which would have meant a much more significant injury.

This year and the prior year had been particularly good years for my golf game. My handicap had come down, I had been to Pebble Beach to play, and was feeling confident about my game. There were many thoughts going through my mind at this time, but one that kept recurring was what effect this would have on my golf game. Broken elbows and golf were not a good match.

X-Rays were taken right away and a brief time later the surgeon on call that night made a visit to my cubicle. The diagnosis was I had a fractured wrist and shattered my right elbow. The surgeon suggested that the operation to fix it be performed right away, that night. He asked if I had any questions, and I did have a couple. The first one was how long I would be out of work and the second was would I be able to play golf again?

The doctor was a boater, not a golfer and gave me a quizzical look. He told me I was fortunate to have not been injured more severely and until he operated and saw the damage, he was not willing to make any promises. Not exactly the comforting words for which I was hoping.

Things moved quickly now, and the next thing I remember was waking up in the recovery room. Whatever pain there was, was numbed by the morphine I had been given and the haze you feel after being under anesthesia. The recovery nurse told me the surgery had gone well but I could feel my arm folded up against my body and it was not going any place soon. I was going to need to learn to do things with my left hand for a time.

The next day the doctor visited to review the surgery. He said I had shattered the elbow ball joint and he had done the best he could to put it back together. He said it would be a couple of months before I could hit a golf ball and said I would need a good stretch of physical therapy to rehab the wrist and elbow.

For the next few months, I walked around being very protective of my arm and elbow. Even when I did not intend it, the arm was tucked up next to my side. It was an inadvertent action which I could not tell I was doing. People did notice and I tried my best not to carry the arm at my side, but I found I frequently did it without even knowing it.

Physical therapy started and it was painful. The work was grueling but right away I was concerned because no matter how much we worked the arm and stretched it, I had lost some range of motion in my right arm. When I returned for my follow up visit, my doctor said that I should start to carry heavy weights around to help with the stretching out process. I did this often and carried anything with weight attached to it around the house with my right arm. I would go into the basement and carry two 25-pound weights by my side to accelerate the process.

No matter what I tried, I could not get the elbow to straighten out. It always had a little bend to it.

Frustration set in and it got worse when I started to hit golf balls. At first with wedges, things seemed fine, but the longer the club the harder it was to make solid contact with the ball. It made me leery to go out and play but I knew I had to if I was going to recover.

I remember the first invitation I accepted to play golf was from a long-time client who I had played with often. It was one of my most painful days on the golf course. Frustrating and embarrassing are words that come to mind too. At a course I had played well at before the fall, I could not even break one hundred. I kept hitting ground balls off the tee and I could not get the ball airborne. There is nothing worse than playing embarrassing bad golf with clients.

I was invited a couple more times with similar results. For someone who loved the game and loved to play, I began to find reasons to turn down invites. The stress and pressure of playing poorly made it not worth playing. It was not fun to play the game like a beginner.

The arm and my golf results did not improve, and I decided to seek out a second opinion. It seemed to me that the results from the surgery should have been better than the range of motion I had. I went to a Boston specialist to see what he thought, but the visit did not offer much hope of improvement. The new surgeon's opinion was that surgery could be done again, but there was no guarantee that things would be any better. The recovery from this operation would be two months, with at least two weeks hooked up to a machine that would move my arm and elbow constantly. This doctor told me that even though the arm was not straight, I was fortunate to have excellent rotary movement of the elbow. He said that he could not guarantee that I would maintain this through the second surgery. Without any kind of guarantee of improvement, it was certainly not worth going through all the pain of surgery again.

Thus, I entered what I would consider my dark days of golf. A long and painful slump.

It lasted a long time, until I met my now wife Tina in 2007.

Now there were certainly rounds of decent play, but I had a really tough time adjusting to the arm and the bend it had. It caused me to hit wild and low hooks and once I started hitting them, it was hard to stop.

During these years I would play golf alone, late in the day at both Sandwich Hollows Golf Course and at Old Barnstable Fairgrounds, courses where I was a member. I would spend hours too, at the driving ranges at both courses, beating balls and hoping to swing my way out of this slump. Ironic, as on the range I would hit it great, but as soon as I got to the course and had to play "real" golf, I was inconsistent and wild. It was not fun, and I was not enjoying playing.

Finally, I knew that if I wanted to keep playing, I needed help. Talking with Tina, I told her that both my boys had attended the David Leadbetter Golf Academy in Bradenton, FL. My parents had a winter place near there and my dad frequently went over to Leadbetter to watch the great young players who trained there work on their games. They did have a weeklong program for adults, so I decided to take the leap and sign up for this program.

It turned out to be money well spent.

It was hard physically, and I hit the most balls I had ever hit in my life. The instructors were knowledgeable and early in the week, they shot video that showed you exactly what you were doing wrong. In a brief period of time, they had my low hard hooks turned into higher softer landing shots.

I did learn that changing a golf swing that you had been making for many years took time to work through. There were still difficulties, but now I at least had a track to run on and I left with much info on my swing and what I needed to work on to play more consistent golf.

The last day was encouraging. We played a round with our instructors coaching us while we played. With my coach reminding me of key points, I hit many good shots and left Leadbetter with hope and a much better attitude about playing. I left too with hands that looked like they had been chopped up pretty well from the thousands of balls I hit that week.

Certainly, the support of Tina helped immensely. Much of our relationship revolved around golf, and I did not want my game to fall apart at this point and let her down.

In the end, there were four important lessons I learned from this experience.

The first, as Winston Churchill said in a famous speech, "never give up and never give in." There were plenty of times I wanted to give up, but golf always seems to draw you back in with that one good shot that makes you think if I can do it once, I can do it every time.

The second lesson was there is no replacement for top quality golf instruction. It is hard to self-diagnose what you are doing with your swing. Having a pro with all the right tools can certainly expedite the learning process. Video is powerful too, and now with everyone having an iPhone, it is easy to see your own swing.

The third lesson was having support. Without my family's and my wife Tina's support and encouragement, I think at some point I may have just given up.

My last lesson was that there is no replacement for playing golf with others and playing for something. One of my favorite things about belonging to Plymouth Country Club is the availability of group play. On every day of the week, you can show up at PCC, put down a couple bucks, and play a game against others. No better way to improve than to play golf when it means something. Even now, Tina and I play a quota match (you get points for eagles, birdies pars and bogies) for small stakes. It is fun to strive to be better and make every shot count even when you are only playing for who buys the ice cream or first cocktail at the bar.

In the end, learning to play with my arm bent has been a journey of patience and persistence. Once in a while when I overdo it (like playing 7 days in a row) I get irritation in the elbow. A day or two of rest and it is back to normal. Considering where I could have ended up with the fall, things have turned out for the best.

In case you are wondering, I am not allowed to climb trees or ladders anymore and if our home needs painting, we will hire someone to do it!

Hole #8

CUPID AND THE MATCH OF A LIFETIME

This story for me started before I even knew it started.

That sentence may need more explaining.

Back in what now seems like another lifetime, a good meaning coworker invited me to a Christmas party at his beautiful home. I was flattered to be invited, but I did not know that there was more to the invite than I expected.

I was recently separated and frankly a mess. I was living in a friend's basement with little extra money, and my self-esteem was at an all-time low. I thought accepting the invite to this party seemed positive on the surface, a chance to get out and be social. Going to the party, however, led to an embarrassing night.

The host had an idea and was honestly trying to help me out. He had a friend who was in a comparable situation to mine and thought it would be a nice opportunity to match me up with her.

I was not prepared or ready for this and was taken by surprise when the true reason for the invitation became apparent.

Lucky for me, my good friend and client Roy Eaton and his lovely wife Rita had been invited to the same party.

After an awkward conversation with the host about his plan, I shuffled over to the Eatons for cover and solace.

They were understanding and I spent much of the evening hiding from the host, planning my escape from the party, and talking to the Eatons about how uncomfortable I was about this situation.

Good does come of bad and that night a seed was planted in the back of Rita Eaton's mind. Rita had a match she thought would be good for me, but given the events at this party, the timing of our meeting needed to be right.

It took time, but the opportunity to meet this match presented itself a few years later when Roy was coming to the end of his illustrious insurance career and was going to retire soon. I was lucky to have access to tickets to a Patriots' game, and not just any tickets, but tickets to a luxury suite. I wanted to do something nice for the Eatons and I knew both were avid Patriots' fans. Since Roy was a principal at one of my highest performing clients, I thought this would be my last chance to invite the Eatons to a game.

So, I did.

It turned out to be a life changing decision.

The luxury suite is a wonderful place to watch a game and with unlimited food and drink it is always a great take. Being in the luxury suite gave us time for conversation. Rita used this time wisely to get vital information from me. She asked about my dating status. One thing for sure about Rita, she was not shy about asking direct questions!

I was not prepared for the question, but it turned out it was right on target. I had gone out on a few dates but so far nothing had come of them. The truth was, I was finding dating challenging to figure out, but I was doing the best I could.

If I needed any convincing, a date early that spring convinced me that I should listen to Rita. It was someone I met on the dating application, Match.com. I thought our first date had gone well and I called a day later to set up a second date. The call did not go like I expected, and I was told flatly, there would be no second date.

I was perplexed that my read of how things went was so far off from her feelings about the date. Against my better judgement, I asked for further clarification on how she made this decision. Her response was blunt. To quote her, "I can tell you are not wild enough for me."

Yikes, that was a punch to the gut.

Stunned, I stammered out the question how in a one-and-a-half-hour dinner could she determine that? Her quick answer was, "I just can." I said thanks and ended the call, but I was certainly perplexed about how I was ever going to navigate this dating thing.

About the same time the ill-fated date had taken place, Rita decided that the timing was right. Her plan had now taken shape and the introduction to the person she had in mind for me to meet would take place at the Hanover Lions Golf Tournament.

The Lions golf event was named The Ted O'Rourke Memorial Golf tournament. The person I would be meeting was Tina O'Rourke. Tina's dad Ted was a long time Lion, avid golfer and had passed away a few years earlier. A number of Tina's family members would be attending, and Tina was playing in a foursome with her brother Kevin and two other close family friends.

At this point Rita needed an ally to pull this off, and there was nobody better than my golfing partner for the day, her husband, Roy. Rita was not playing golf in the tournament, and it would be up to Roy to make sure our meeting took place.

I know Rita gave Roy detailed instructions about how things should go on the big day. It was a major responsibility for him to make sure the meeting took place before golf started. This was particularly important to Tina because she told Rita she did not want the meeting to happen after golf when she would have "hat head."

My first instruction from Roy was I needed to get to the course early. I assured Roy that was no issue, and I knew that the golf course had a range and I always like to hit a few balls before playing. Once I got to the range there were a couple people warming up. I was wondering if the woman hitting balls near me was Tina, but that thought was interrupted when Roy arrived and found me.

Clearly Rita had put the pressure on Roy not to screw this up and once he found me at the range the frantic search to find Tina was on. I pointed out the woman at the range and got an irritated no from Roy.

So off we went to comb the parking lot, starting area and carts to find Tina. The search did not go well, and I could see the increasing stress in Roy's face as time was slipping by. Turns out there were issues on Tina's end getting to the event.

Tina was coming to the event with her brother Kevin, and Kevin is a notorious "trunk slammer." A trunk slammer in golf is someone who barely makes their tee time and normally slams the trunk shut as they rush to the first tee. Kevin was one of the best at this and had it down to a tee.

Knowing Kevin's "trunk slammer" tendencies, Tina implored Kevin to be ready on time because she needed to get to the golf event on the early side this year. It may have helped if Kevin had known what was going on, but he was not in the know on the "meeting" plan. Once a trunk slammer always a trunk slammer and like always Kevin was running late. Even though Roy and I were diligently looking for Tina, she was not even on the property yet!

I could see the stress mounting in Roy as Rita was checking in on progress and the shotgun start tee time was rapidly approaching. Roy grabbed my arm and told me we should head up to the clubhouse to see if Tina was hanging out there. She was not in the clubhouse, and we had given up hope on the meeting happening before the shotgun start. When we dejectedly headed over to find our cart, we ran right into Tina as she was rushing to find her cart as well.

Roy's face was a picture of relief. He happily made the introduction. Mission accomplished!

Tina and I exchanged small talk about golf and what a lovely day it was. Tina did mention that there was a number of family members and friends at the tournament and that she was sorry she was late. I remember making a comment about Tina's pullover when suddenly the call came for all of us to head to our carts for the start of the event. We parted and I hoped to talk with Tina again after the golf.

Roy peppered me with "what did you think" questions and I am sure Rita wanted immediate feedback. Tina seemed lovely and I thought the few minutes had gone well. Luckily, the round started, and the questions and tension subsided.

That was until the golf was finished.

When we took our place at the outdoor picnic tables for lunch and prize awards, Roy had an idea. Tina had come in and was sitting at a table with her mother Annie, her brothers Kevin and Rob and what looked like a bevy of long time Hanover friends.

Roy instructed me that I should leave our table and teammates and head over to the O'Rourke table. I took another look at the table and knew there was no way in hell I was going over there. I did not know a single person at the table. Tina's mom Annie looked to be holding court with the group and they were all talking, laughing, and having a "large" time. I could just picture things grinding to a halt at the O'Rourke table as a stranger (me) invaded their fun. Roy again insisted that he thought I should slide over to their table and again I looked over and thought no way am I walking cold into that scene.

I was nervous and was trying to think of a way out of this situation quickly. I had an idea and suggested an alternative to Roy, which might put a little less pressure on me. I floated my thought to Roy that if Tina agreed, we would meet for dinner at a later date and have a more relaxed introduction. After getting the all-important approval from Rita, Roy said it was ok and Rita would coordinate the dinner plans.

A big sigh of relief for me!

A couple of weeks later the first real date took place. The dinner went smoothly and once we were finished eating, the Eatons excused themselves and left us to talk. There was sports, family and college football talk and we agreed to meet again.

The next meeting was not as smooth as the dinner. I had Red Sox tickets and invited Tina to attend the game with me. The only problem was I had meetings in Keene, NH that day and unfortunately the meetings lasted longer than expected.

My traveling companion on many Keene trips was my good friend and co-worker Elaine Cedrone who bailed me out by calling her husband and had him meet us at a rest stop on Route 24 in Bridgewater, MA. Otherwise, I was never going to make it to Boston for the date and game.

It was still going to be close and at this point I did not have Tina's cell phone number. I drove ninety miles per hour up Route 3 and squeezed through multiple yellow lights. I found a parking spot quickly and ran up Jersey Street to our meeting place. Tina told me later that she was getting nervous waiting because I was a little late. Tina had the thought that I was standing her up and she was thinking of leaving. I was thankful she hung in there for that few extra minutes.

We made our way into the park and decided we would have Fenway Franks for dinner. Our conversation came easily, and we talked more about jobs, sports, and families. I had four seats but there was a threat of rain and the two other guests decided to blow off the game and did not attend. I was disappointed with them, but we did enjoy the extra room this gave us.

The big moment of the night came after the game ended and we were leaving the park. We were walking towards where my car was parked, and Tina told me she would be fine taking a taxi home. Tina further explained that she knew I lived in Sandwich and already had a long ride home without going out of my way to her place in West Roxbury. I told Tina that while I appreciated her concern, I would not feel right not making sure she got home safely. After a brief discussion, she begrudgingly gave in. It was the right thing to do, and I think I may have earned points for making sure she got home without any issues. Not sure I got a kiss good night, but points earned were good enough for now!

The story has a happy conclusion. Through the busy summer and fall we managed to find time to be with each other and the relationship started to grow and blossom.

Sometime during our courtship Rita was given the nickname Cupid. A nickname I know she loves, and she is immensely proud of the good match she made for Tina and me. We were married on 9/22/2012 and golf has remained a large part of our lives. We have played hundreds of rounds together, taken exciting golf trips, won a golf tournament on the same team, and joined a golf club together. Golf has been a strong bond right from our first meeting.

Since our match was a success, many have asked Cupid why she did not make any more matches after ours. Her reply has always been "I am batting 1000 and that is the way I want to keep it."

We are both thankful for what Rita and Roy did for us.

In the end, Cupid knew best!

Hole #9

IRISH ENGAGEMENT

The perfect Irish name is O'Rourke
And the equally perfect place
For an Irish girl to get engaged,
is County Cork!

So, my little Irish poem is not the quality writing of the great Irish poets like Yeats or my friend John Hopkins. What does exist in that little ditty is an idea that had been percolating in my mind for some time. Where would be the perfect place for an Irish girl to get engaged?

Tina O'Rourke, my Irish lass, and I had been together now for three years. Things were progressing well, and we were enjoying being together. Things were going so well that I started to have thoughts about the M word, marriage. Something I never thought I would do again now seemed a possibility.

If I had any doubts (which I did not), my family and friends who met Tina were wowed by her. They loved her easy way, quick laugh and how she made people who she just met seem like old friends.

One memory that really drove this point home to me happened during a Liberty Mutual trip with a group of my clients to Florida. Tina joined me on this trip. The trip was a prize for a contest I had won while employed at Liberty Mutual, and the trip was important. The senior management team from Liberty would be present and we would be attending a cocktail party with them. I would receive a prestigious award from the President of our company during the party. I was thrilled to have Tina with me on this trip to share the moment and help me deal with the stress of the week.

My friend and client Wayne Guyer was on the trip too with his wife Jean. Jean and Tina had spent an afternoon together doing one of the planned activities, a bike trip around South Beach. They had a blast and enjoyed each other's company.

That same night, Tina and I were hosting a table for the week- ending celebration. It was a large time with great food, live music, and dancing. Wayne and Jean were guests at our table. Jean came over to me before the dinner and asked if she could have a quick word. I assumed there was something about the week or event she wanted to discuss, but I assumed wrong. Jean's words were direct and straightforward. She said "I am not sure how you found Tina, but if you are smart you will never let her get away. She is an absolute gem!"

A bit flustered, I stammered out that I agreed, and I promised I would not let her get away. It was an interesting admission for me that I just blurted out. It was clear to everyone I knew and to me, that it was close to the time to take the big step and "put a ring on it" like Beyonce says.

Sometimes the best laid plans fall in place naturally. That was certainly the case with what happened with my plans with Tina for the Irish Engagement.

The plan began to take shape a short time later with discussions with my brother Mark and his wife Donna about a golf trip to Ireland with Tina and me. Mark had been with a group of his fellow CPA firm partners before for a 40th birthday celebration for one of his business partners. Mark thought the trip was terrific and all the courses were outstanding. This trip was something Tina and I wanted to do, and we started to search out dates. It is always a challenge to get everyone's calendar aligned.

After some discussion, we decided to head to the Southwest section of Ireland in September of 2010. There are many top-notch courses to choose from in the southwest and all the ones we picked were top 100 courses in the world. Tralee, Ballybunion, Waterville, Lahinch and last but not least, Old Head. Not a weak course in the group and Old Head looked like an incredibly special place.

An important part of Tina's job was coordinating complicated travel for the people she worked with. She was exceptional at it but for this trip it was unfair to have her be involved in the details of planning a vacation trip in her free time. It was too much like what she did at work every day. I volunteered to manage the travel part knowing I better get it right as she was a stickler for details. I know she really appreciated me doing it though.

When the trip got closer, I started to put my engagement plan in place. First, I would need a ring. My friend from Sandwich, MA, Eric Hokanson, had a family connection with a diamond dealer. I made an appointment with the diamond dealer, and he had picked out four beautiful diamonds for me to view. They all had their strong points, and I was torn between two.

I called my good friend from work, Linda Durkin, and told her about the two choices. Linda made it easy and told me straight out that I better pick the larger one of the two as "bigger is always better." I listened to Linda and followed her advice and was pleased with my choice.

I picked up the ring a week prior to the trip on a day I was playing golf with three of my longtime work friends, Roy Eaton, Elaine Cedrone and Laura Nicholas. When I arrived at the course, I realized I had to do something with the ring. I could not leave it in the car, so the ring found a temporary home tucked in the pocket of my golf bag that was designed for my wallet. I checked the pocket frequently fearing the ring would somehow manage to fall out of the bag.

I was excited about my plans, but I had not shared my plan with anyone yet other than Linda and Eric. That changed this day, and my three friends were the first to know the entire plan. This was especially important to my friend Roy as he would now have a "scoop" on his wife Rita (aka Cupid our matchmaker from a prior story). Rita always got any news about what was going on with Tina and me before Roy. I knew Roy would relish the moment when he got home and was able to drop this bombshell news on Rita! The two of them were quite comical about being "in the know" about what Tina and I were up to. They certainly both had a personal stake in our engagement.

Since I now had told a limited group of friends, it was time to tell my two sons, Erik, and Kurt. They had come to know Tina over the past three years, and she bonded with them one day when she was at my house for a visit. The boys were out in the street shooting baskets and Tina headed out to join them. She was not afraid to get into the mix and make a couple hoops. I was nervous telling them about my plan, but it went well, and they were happy for me.

Prior to the trip I did research about the different courses we would be visiting, and which one would be the best match for the site of the Irish Engagement. It became a clear and easy choice. It would be Old Head for two good reasons.

First, Old Head was our first planned golf stop. I did not want to spend the whole trip worrying about losing the ring!

Secondly, Old Head was a special site with interesting history. During my research about Old Head, I learned about the land's history and the significance of the two Stones of Accord they had on their property.

One of the Stones of Accord was located next to the putting green and the other was out on the golf course. The Stone's history dated back to the times before Christ. Up until the 17th century, they were used to seal an important deal or reconcile after an argument. The Stones of Accord were also used to seal wedding vows.

My decision was made. Old Head would be the perfect spot for the Irish Engagement which would take place at one of the Stones of Accord.

Our travel day to Ireland finally came, and our plan was for me to pick up Tina at her place in West Roxbury and we would drive to the airport together. I should have planned better given Tina's diligence and punctuality. Due to heavy traffic, I was running late. I arrived at her place and there was my soon to be fiancé sitting on her suitcase outside, on her porch. She clearly was displeased with my tardiness, especially since she emphatically told me how she always wanted to be at the airport early when she flew. Thankfully, traffic was light on this part of our ride, and we arrived at Logan Airport right on time.

Once we got the car parked, Tina caught me off guard with an unexpected request. Being a seasoned traveler, she had a few sundries that she wanted to put in my carry- on bag just in case her suitcase was lost. I choked on this request because the engagement ring was hidden in the bottom of my carry- on bag. I quickly replied "no." There was no way I would want her fishing around in my carry-on and finding the ring by accident. She shot me a confused look and later told me she just chalked it up to me being very territorial and we would operate on a "what is mine is mine and yours is yours basis."

The flight was on time, and we arrived in Shannon at 5 am. We gathered our luggage and clubs and stepped out into a fine Irish mist (pouring rain) for our three-hour drive over to the lovely little village of Kinsale. Even though we were tired we knew we had to stay awake to adjust to the time change.

We found a scenic nine-hole course called Ringanon, just outside town to play a warmup round. My brother Mark tore the course up with multiple birdies and we visited the clubhouse and all in the bar were in a jovial mood seeing that Cork was winning the Irish Football Championship that day. Our new friends in the bar were so happy with the trend of the game that they bought us our first Murphy's Irish Stout of the trip. There would be a few more!

Day two was our day to head out to Old Head. Mark had told us the story from his prior trip about the course being fogged in and unplayable. The cliffs in some spots were over 300 feet high off the water and rocks. With foul weather and poor visibility there could be a chance of people stumbling off the cliff by accident. Needless to say, we were praying for good weather.

There was one small detail I needed to take care of that morning. I had not told Donna and Mark about the plan for the engagement. Luckily, Tina needed a little extra time to primp in the room that morning and I let the secret out at breakfast before Tina's arrival. Donna and Mark were happy for me, and we had to curtail the discussion when Tina joined us in the breakfast room.

Arriving at Old Head is quite the sight with the spit of land jutting out into the Atlantic visible as you drive down the long access road. During WW 1 the Lusitania was torpedoed a few miles off this point and this was the last piece of land the passengers of the Titanic saw on their ill-fated voyage. The weather was cool and breezy with just a light wind. Thank God no fog.

The views and scenery were impressive and there was no doubt you needed to watch your step on the narrow goat paths you walked along on the course. There were signs everywhere telling you to stay back from the edges of the cliffs or risk a long fall and certain death. The Old Head cliffs were the highest I had ever seen on a golf course. They made for spectacular and dramatic golf holes!

I was not sure when we would be near the Stones of Accord, so the ring was in my golf bag again. This time it was in my golf ball pocket. I was checking it once a hole. The round was fun, and the weather got better with blue sky and sun breaking through when we headed to the back nine.

There is so much to see, that the impending engagement had slipped to the back of my mind. That was until the 17th hole when Donna brought me back down to earth.

When we were walking to our drives down the right side of the long par 5 17th hole, Donna strolled over to me and asked, "getting nervous yet?" To that point I was not, but all of a sudden, I was.

To prove the nerves had set in, I hit a huge slice on my next shot that ended up miles out into the Atlantic. By far, the worst shot I hit all day. 17 was a beautiful hole and I was mad about the poor shot. I dropped another ball and tried again. Same result. I think the reality of what was going to happen soon was setting in.

We arrived at the 18th hole, and we all walked back to the championship tee which was perched on a small cliff. Not a place you would want to lose your balance, but an amazing view and tee shot to try.

Tina made a huge splash on the 18th green by rolling in a bomb of a putt from forty feet for a birdie. It was a terrific way to finish the round. If I was nervous on 17, I was super nervous now. The time for the big question was now rapidly approaching.

I had noticed from the 18th green that the Stone of Accord that was on the golf course was going to be a long walk from the clubhouse. After walking eighteen holes, I did not think Tina would go for that spot. It was going to have to be the Stone of Accord by the putting green for the big proposal. Now I needed a quick plan to get Tina back over to the putting green.

While we headed to our vehicle to store our clubs, I decided I needed to act quickly. I told Tina that I wanted us to have a picture at the Stone. It was a short walk from the car but Tina, wanting to be inclusive, asked Donna and Mark if they wanted to come along. At this point they knew what was going to happen and said no but they would meet us in the Lusitania Bar in the clubhouse.

After a short walk down a path and across the putting green we arrived at the spot and the decisive moment. I had been able to sneak the ring out of my bag and into my pocket and managed to get down on one knee when we arrived at the Stone. At first, I am not sure Tina knew what I was doing and was concerned because it looked like I had fallen. Then she saw the box and the sparkle of the diamond, and I knew I had surprised her. Tina's face began to light up with a huge smile, and I could see the beginning of tears coming from her bright blue eyes.

I was able to get the "will you marry me" words out and Tina's response was "Of Course!" Words that we repeated on our wedding day during our vows because it was such a natural response.

It was quiet and serene around the putting green which made the whole scene quite special. After Tina said "of course" we shook hands thru the Stone of Accord. At this same time, we both realized that there was not a soul around to take a picture of us. All of a sudden, we heard this lyrical Irish voice say softly with his brogue "aye, I believe I just witnessed something special happen here!" My words do not do justice to the sound we remember of his sweet voice.

Turns out he was the golf course starter, and he had been watching us through the window of his stone hut. He was so kind and such a godsend as we wanted to have a couple of pictures taken. It certainly made an emotional moment even more emotional for Tina because our starter friend did remind her of her dad who had passed away a few years' prior. It was like he was there with us.

We headed back to the clubhouse, where Mark and Donna were waiting. The emotions caught up with Tina again when she saw them, and she started to cry. Donna shot me a look as if to say what happened and then in her normal direct style said to Tina "why are you crying, did you say no?" We still laugh about that line to this day and Tina's answer was "of course not!"

There were still a few tears so Donna showed Tina the way to the lady's locker room so she could "compose herself." Things settled down and we had a delicious lunch and pictures outside on the deck. Mark was directing the picture taking and was not satisfied with how they were coming out. He told us emphatically "make like you like each other!" With that Tina slapped her ring hand across my chest to show off the ring. We both had huge smiles on our faces and Mark snapped at the exact right moment to catch it. It is one of my favorite pictures ever taken of the two of us and the memories of that day make me smile every time I see it.

After lunch we headed back to our hotel. Another small detail I missed in my planning was that neither Tina nor I had a cell phone with us. There were quite a few people who would be excited to hear the news and we had no way to tell them. Good thing someone was thinking; Mark had international service on his phone, so he was nice enough to let us borrow it and we retreated to our room to make calls.

The funniest of those was to our friends Rita (Cupid) and Roy Eaton who were responsible for us meeting. They were excited to hear the news but our time talking to them was limited. They were on vacation in Disney World and about to take off on the Kali River Rapids water ride. No place for a cell phone to be out.

The next morning at breakfast at our hotel Blindgate House, we told the proprietor Maeve our good news. She asked Tina if she could try on the ring. This, Maeve told us, was an Irish custom that was supposed to bring on good luck to the couple (it worked).

We had a wonderful week in Ireland and the good luck from Maeve trying on the ring must have spilled over to golf. We experienced gale force winds at Tralee, but only a tiny bit of rain at the beginning of our round at Waterville. Our group was fortunate to have such pleasant weather and hardly any rain. Tina was able to show off the ring every place we went, and it was nice to relax for the week and enjoy the engagement celebration.

The only question still open from the trip is… was Tina more excited about making the long putt for birdie on the 18th at Old Head or getting the engagement ring minutes later? I know the answer, but I tease her all the time that I think the birdie may have been a bigger deal!

HALFWAY HOUSE

Enjoy a hot dog, a beer and my Chip Shot Stories

Chip Shots

SHORT STORIES FROM "A LIFE ABOVE PAR"

FIRST TEE BLUES

Everyone who plays the game has experienced a wayward shot or two off the first tee. I think of the thousands of good shots I have hit to start a round, and I can hardly remember any of them.

Clear as day, I can remember my two most disastrous first tee shots.

Number one took place at the new Wollaston Golf Course in Milton, MA. It was the first time I had ever played the course and I was playing with a new client (a father and son) and a co-worker. I was excited because I had been a caddie there back when the course was in Quincy and always had wanted to play the new Wollaston.

The first hole is a little funky and is a sharp dogleg left and downhill. My host had warned me that I may not need to hit my driver on this hole due to the sharp dogleg. Heeding his advice, I decided to hit my five wood.

I was nervous and swung quickly and hit the ball right off the toe of the club. The ball traveled about six feet to the right and bounced off a wooden split rail fence to the right of me. The ball came back to rest a foot from where I stood. My partners all had a roaring laugh and were nice enough to let me hit another one, but it was such an awful feeling to see that ball at my feet.

The second one was at the Woods Hole Country Club on Cape Cod. Again, I was the guest of a client and playing with two other guests. In this case, I had not been playing much and was not hitting the ball consistently.

The first hole at Woods Hole is a short par four. I decided to hit my three wood.

I hit a ground ball that hit off the white tee marker in front of me and it shot up in the air over my head and into an unplayable lie out of bounds behind the tee. My host said he had never seen anyone pull off a shot like that!

I wanted to die.

The rest of the day was not much better but thankfully my client invited me back a few years later and I was able to redeem myself.

Most times now I hit a driver off the first tee. With the enormous size of the driver clubhead nowadays, there is less chance I will miss like I did above!

LOST BALL

I had a different kind of golf experience watching my son Erik play in an American Junior Golf Association qualifier. We were at the Eisenhower Park Golf Complex on Long Island, NY.

Erik was playing the front nine and I was trying to stay out of the way and help find any wayward shots his group hit. When I was watching Erik on the 3rd hole, I had an interesting encounter with one of his competitors who was playing the adjacent 17th hole.

From where I was standing, I heard a ball hit from the 17th tee land in the tall grass near where I was. I walked over and found the ball. To mark it, I put my hat down where the ball was and waited while the group approached me.

The player who hit the shot came over to me and was thankful that I had found his ball. He said he was playing well and thought he had a chance to qualify for the tournament. What he said next shocked me and made me sad.

He told me most parents he had encountered at these events would not have helped find the ball. His rationale was that everyone playing was competing for limited spots in the tournament. He told me by helping him, I could be hurting my own son's chances to qualify. He nodded towards another parent following his group and said, "that guy there would have stepped on the ball if he found it."

I was stunned by the statement and replied to him that I thought helping him was in the spirit of what the game was about.

He shot me a wry smile, and said, "maybe that's what you think, but most parents here only care about their own kid and getting them into the tournament."

I'm not sure I believed him, but it was certainly a cynical attitude for a 16-year-old kid to have. I will always remember how surprised and thankful he was that I found his ball.

DONALD ROSS GOLF COURSES

Donald Ross was one of the premier golf architects of his time. After coming to this country from Scotland, he had his first job in the US at Oakley Country Club in Watertown, MA. Ross lived and worked too at Essex County Club in Manchester-by-the Sea, MA. Ross was a busy man,

building golf courses across the country with a heavy concentration on the east coast.

Here in Massachusetts, there are thirty-nine Ross designs that are still open and active. Of the thirty-nine, I have
been fortunate to play thirty of them. My goal is to play
every one in MA, and I am proud that my home course,
Plymouth Country Club, is a Donald Ross design.

I enjoy the way that Ross routed his courses. His courses
were constructed before the advent of large earth moving
machines and he needed to mold the design of his holes
into the terrain of the land, for a natural look.

Ross greens are always a challenge, and if you can play
a round on one of his designs and not three putt, you have
accomplished something. He is certainly my favorite golf
architect and I love the playability of his designs.

PASATIEMPO GOLF COURSE

It is hard to call this course underrated because it does
make all the lists of top golf courses you can play. I am always surprised that people have not heard of it or miss stopping at Pasatiempo on the way to or from Pebble Beach. It
sits about halfway between Pebble and San Francisco on
the coast in the town of Santa Cruz.

What makes Pasatiempo worth the stop?

It is one of the few courses designed by Alister Mackenzie (architect of Augusta National and Cypress Point) that is
open to the public. The holes are beautifully bunkered, and
the greens reminded me of the tricky Donald Ross greens
at my home course. One hole is reminiscent of the 18th at
Augusta with its tree lined tee shot.

McKenzie lived just off the sixth hole and spent the last
years of his life living in this house. Pasatiempo is not an

inexpensive place to play but worth it for the experience and history.

PLAYING CAPE COD

When I moved to Cape Cod back in 1985, I set a goal to play every course on the Cape. It took over 35 years to accomplish this feat, and it took a bit of luck to get on all the private courses.

It helped to have clients that were members of the private courses on the Cape, many of whom were kind enough to invite me to play. The Osterville Free Library Tournament helped me get on both Wianno and Oyster Harbors where I did not have any contacts. I was fortunate to get invites to all the private courses and it just took time to get to all the public ones.

During the first year of Covid, with my wife Tina and good friend Laura Nicholas, I planned a fun trip to get the last course in. That course was Chatham Seaside Links right next to the Chatham Bars Inn in Chatham, MA. We combined playing this last course I needed with two other Cape Cod classics, Highland Links in Truro and Chequessett Yacht & Country Club in Wellfleet, MA. Both are enjoyable courses to walk and play. They are about the closest to links golf that you can get in this part of the country.

It was a terrific way to end a long and fun quest, and the great picture Laura took that day at Highland Links graces the cover of this book.

A DUNK FOR A WIN

My son Erik played a heavy schedule of competitive junior golf in his high school years. Some events allowed parents to walk along and watch, and some did not. Watching your child play tournament golf is not an easy thing. There were times I thought I was better off not watching because my presence seemed a distraction. No more so than at the Massachusetts Junior Amateur at Red Tail Golf Course when I showed up near the end of the round, to see Erik's last two holes. His only two bogies of the final round.

On the Titleist Junior Tour, parents were not allowed on the course. On this day this was fine with me, as the course he was playing, Far Corners Golf Course in Boxford, MA, had a 9-hole course that I could play while the event was going on.

Far Corners had a deck that overlooked the 18th hole, and I was able to get back in time to watch Erik finish. The good news was the deck was out of sight and Erik would not be able to see me.

I had no idea how he was playing as there were no scoreboards, but when his group hit their drives on eighteen, one hit off a large tree down the right side. I could see two others in the fairway, but as luck would have it, it was Erik's ball that hit the tree. It looked like he may have had to chip out, but from where I was standing it was hard to tell.

Things happened quickly now, and I could see Erik hit his next shot. I tried to follow it, and luckily looked towards the green just when the ball took one bounce, hit the flag stick, and went in! An unlikely shot but it was a thing of beauty.

I met Erik after the round just off the green and asked what he had made on 18. He said a birdie and he thought it was going to be one of his lowest rounds ever.

We headed inside so he could tally his score. When the score was posted with the help of the birdie on 18, Erik had won the event by one shot. It was his first time under par in a tournament and first time I had ever seen him win. It was an amazing golf moment for both of us.

A VOTE FOR PLAYING ALONE

Golf is a great social game and there is no doubt that playing with others is an important part of the game. Saying that, once in a while I just like to take a walk and play alone.

Instead of going to the range and beating balls, I now practice when I play alone. I use this time to hit shots I would actually hit during a round. It could be just me, but I must have hit millions of balls at driving ranges and never seemed to improve. Playing the course alone and practicing this way seems to work for me and my handicap is at an all-time low.

The majority of the times I do this, it is late in the day and our course is quiet and peaceful. There is a certain joy in hitting shots and being able to walk slowly and enjoy the surroundings.

My favorite time for this is in the evening in the summer. The breeze is cooler, the sun is setting and often times the wind dies down. For me, it is a perfect way to unwind and end a day.

AN UNDERRATED FORMAT

Tuesday night is my favorite night at my home course. Tuesday is our nine-hole quota match, called TNT, short for Tuesday Night Twilight.

What makes quota so good? It is a format that I play against myself and my handicap. It is all on me and if I make a birdie or two, there is a chance to get in the money.

It is a profitable event for our club too, as on Tuesday night when the dining room would be quiet, it is full of members having dinner and drinks waiting for the winners to be announced when all the players are finished.

It is a popular format in Scotland and Ireland, and I wish we would use it more in our major club events. It sure beats the five plus hour stroke play tournament rounds that we have each summer.

DOWN GOES K-ROB

My son Kurt and I had never played in a tournament together, and we decided to try it when we were both members at Old Barnstable Fairgrounds. We entered the fall member- member tournament as a team.

The first day did not go well and neither of us could get things going. Our poor play earned us an early tee time on day two.

Things improved the second day, and we played the front nine much better than on day one. We were not going to win the tournament, but we were going to make up ground on the field.

We made the turn and hit our drives on the 10th hole. Kurt hit his down the tree line on the right side of the hole. The ball came to rest a few yards in back of a large tree. It looked like Kurt had a shot if he could hook the ball around the tree. Since we had no chance of winning, we figured why not go for it.

Kurt took a mighty swing and scorched one. Unfortunately, it was straight and hit the tree dead center. Before he could even react, the ball ricocheted hard off the tree right back at him and hit him square in the mouth!

Down he went in a heap, and when I got over to him there was blood gushing out of his mouth. All I could think of was that he had broken all his front teeth.

When we got the blood washed away, we could see that it was not the teeth, but he had bitten down on his tongue and taken a huge gash out of it.

We told our partners that we would need to withdraw, and off to the hospital we went. A quick check by the emergency room doctor showed no major damage, but the unwelcome news was that nothing could be done for a cut on the tongue.

This diagnosis of Kurt's injury was followed by a couple of weeks of careful eating. Certainly, it was a shot we will never forget.

GEORGE PEPER

While there are scores of great golf writers, if I could meet one it would be George Peper. I have enjoyed his writings in *Links Magazine* for years, and his book called *Two Years in St. Andrews* is one of my favorites.

When we visited St Andrews a few years ago we did try to find his house that was located adjacent to the 18th hole. We realized at the end of the week we had been looking at the wrong house, but I am sure the occupants did not mind us waving at them as we walked down the 18th fairway every day.

His column in *Links* about his 750 courses played inspired me to go back and count all of the courses I have played (right now at 400). Another column by Peper I enjoyed is his list of one hundred things everyone should do in golf. I have done sixty of the things on his list, but I have realized there are one or two items that may be out of reach for me.

A work friend's family are good friends with Mr. Peper, and they forwarded on an email I sent them with the list and the number of his "things" I had done. He replied that I was doing well and encouraged me to keep at it.

I kept the email and someday I will get up the courage to invite Mr. Peper to play Plymouth Country Club with me. I have no doubt it would be enjoyable, and I am sure I would ask tons of questions and be an attentive listener. One thing I would suggest to him would be to add playing with a famous author as the 101st thing you should do in golf.

GONE BUT NOT FORGOTTEN

Last March, my wife Tina and I headed over to Bryant University to watch her nephew Marc O'Rourke play lacrosse. When we were leaving, I asked Tina if she would mind driving a mile out of our way to see if the Smithfield Driving Range was still in business.

When we arrived, it was apparent that the range no longer existed. It looked like the land had been sold to build houses.

Back in the late 1980's, I got to know the former owners Guido and Frances DeSalvo during my time as a Premium Auditor for CNA Insurance.

My audit of their sales records took about ten minutes to complete, and I would spend many hours talking to the DeSalvo's about golf, golf travel and equipment. I gained valuable insights about golf from my visits with them.

I looked forward to seeing them every year. One year they convinced me that my clubs needed to be upgraded and they sold me a set of Ping Eye Two Golf Clubs. I still have the majority of this set 35 years later and both my boys have used the Pings as a starter set of clubs.

Guido passed away in 2015 and the range was in business for 48 years. They were kind and interesting people, and I will never forget them.

PAR 3 UNDER THE LIGHTS

A big trip for our family in the summer when I was growing up would be to West Bridgewater to Bunceys Par 3. I drove by the site recently, and it had sadly fallen into disrepair.

Bunceys was an 18-hole par three course with holes that varied from a length of fifty yards to over one hundred yards. They had go-carts too, but normally we would just play golf.

In those days it was a big night out for our family. It was especially exciting when it got dark, and the lights would come on. Golf at night was a unique experience.

My mother, Marjorie Robinson, had her greatest golf moment at Bunceys when a shot she hit went into the hole on the fly for a hole in one! My mom was not a golfer, but she never let us forget that she was the first one in the family with a hole in one.

I returned to Bunceys frequently with my high school friends, and we would go to experience golf under the lights.

I am not sure why but after at least thirty years in business it closed in 2015. I have fond memories from playing there and I am sad to see it gone.

FAVORITE MATCH

Every year I play a few matches against my good friend Laura Nicholas. Laura and I worked together for about fifteen years until I moved on to another job and company. We have stayed friends ever since.

Laura is highly competitive and each time we play we have a match. Unlike most matches though, we only play for bragging rights till the next match. No money, just pride on the line.

All but one or two of the matches have come right down to the last hole and last putt. Laura is really tough to beat at her home course, Braintree Municipal.

I always know I need to bring my "A" game when I play Laura, since I know she always brings hers. Laura always makes me play better!

FINAL THOUGHTS

Nothing kills a round of golf like slow play.

Why is it so difficult for people to rake bunkers?

Beer always tastes better after a round of golf.

THE BACK 9

Hole #10

LATE NIGHT MULLIGAN AT ST ANDREWS

There are many great finishing holes in golf. The walk up the 18th hole at Pebble Beach or the 18th hole at Pinehurst #2 come to mind as a couple of my favorites. To me though, there is no better stroll in golf than the walk up the 18th at the Old Course in St Andrews, Scotland.

It may not be the most scenic, but it is certainly the most historic with all the great players in the history of golf walking those same steps as you do when you play the Old Course. It also has the most famous bridge in golf, The Swilcan Bridge, where every group always pauses to pose for pictures.

Certainly, one of the most unique features of the Old Course is that it becomes a public park on Sunday and no golf is allowed. When Tina and I arrived in St Andrews for the first time together, it was a Sunday. We came around the corner to find Rusacks Hotel and could not believe the scene that laid out in front of us. We saw people with blankets having picnics, dogs chasing thrown sticks, and soccer balls being kicked. It certainly helped that we arrived in St Andrews in the middle of an epic heat wave, and it was a perfect Sunday to be outside enjoying the Old Course and fine weather.

When we started our trip, we were not sure if we would get to play the Old Course. In the planning portion of the trip, we were unable to secure a tee time but luckily there are alternative ways to play the Old.

The one hope we had was to have success with the daily lottery called The Ballot. The Ballot is something I wrote about in a prior story and is another unique feature of the Old Course. Spots are held open each day for the general public and through The Ballot you can enter the drawing every day for one of the coveted tee times. From what I had read, there was a twenty five percent chance of getting a tee time with this method.

If The Ballot did not work, there was always the opportunity to get up early and get into the "walk on" line. Tina was not enthused about this option because it meant being up exceedingly early in the morning and standing outside for an extended period of time in the dark and cold.

The day before our flight left for Scotland, I was in my home office and remembered that our first chance at The Ballot had been drawn that day. I jumped on the website and let out a loud scream when I saw our names on the Old Course tee sheet. Tina yelled up to me thinking I had hurt myself. I said I was fine and that we just got exciting news. That news being we would be playing the Old Course our second day in Scotland. I could not believe our good luck.

The weather remained amazingly warm and all the servers at Rusacks had sunburns from heading to the beach to enjoy the great weather. We loved Rusacks Hotel and we had breakfast every morning overlooking the first and eighteenth fairways of the Old Course. Tina was struck with the pure joy she saw from golfers walking down the first fairway sometimes hugging each other and laughing with immense joy knowing they were starting one of the most anticipated rounds of their lives.

Soon, it was our turn. The day of our tee time arrived, and we started the day like always, watching group after group head down the first fairway. This morning we ate breakfast quickly, as we wanted to be over to the first tee early just to make sure everything went right.

The practice range at St Andrews is a long way from the first tee of the Old Course, so we decided we would just loosen up and putt prior to our round. We presented our handicap cards, paid our greens fee, and met our partners for the day, two Americans.

We all managed good drives on the super wide first hole, and off we went with our four caddies to do our best to bring the Old Course to its knees.

One of the highlights for both of us that day took place at the 12th hole called Heathery In. It is a shorter par four hole that the professionals try to drive during The Open. It only plays 316 yards from the regular tees. It looks like a benign hole at first look, but there is trouble all over that you cannot see from the tee.

There are sand traps that are hidden from sight and the best place to be with your tee shot is the left side of the fairway. It is hard to see the green from the left, but if you are on this side you are away from the traps and will have a clean shot to the green.

Tina hit a nice drive down the left side and it stopped in a safe spot. I did not listen well enough to our caddies and hit one down the right side and caught the last bunker.

Since I was on the right side, I walked a little ahead of our group to check out the green and was glad I did.

The green on twelve is different from all of the others on the Old Course as it has two tiers. The day we played it the pin was on the front tier of the green.

When Tina hit her shot, it landed short of the green and then went on a wild ride. It broke from right to left and caught the slope. It managed to catch the slope perfectly and was making a beeline right at the pin. It rolled right past the flag and stopped an inch from the hole. A tap in birdie!

Unfortunately, Tina saw none of this as her view of the green was blocked by one of the many humps and bumps of the Old Course. She could see I was excited, and she was too when she got over the crest of the bump and could see the great result and her easy birdie putt.

My shot was not as dramatic, but it was not an easy one. I needed to clear the lip of the bunker from about seventy yards out and stop the ball on the correct level. I was happy to get my shot over the lip of the bunker and on to the front of the green and two putt for a nice par.

The exciting thing about this part of the round is you have made the turn back towards the town and now can see it growing closer on every shot. You know you have tough holes coming in, the huge Hell Bunker on the par five 14th, the famous Principal's Nose Bunker on the 16th and the 17th, the difficult Road Hole.

The Road Hole is known as one of the hardest par fours in the world. It is certainly the only hole that you need to hit a drive over an old railroad barn to find the fairway. The hole is the longest par four on the course, and the green looks like a sliver when you stare down your second shot and try to make sure you miss the dangerous Road Hole Bunker guarding the left side of the green.

After a short walk from the 17th green, you come to the end of your round and have the largest fairway in golf to hit your drive. The fairway is 129 yards wide and has an active road, Grannie Clark's Wynd, that runs through it. Common advice is to aim for the clock on the Royal & Ancient clubhouse on your drive.

Our foursome approached the 18th and one of our playing partners went first. He had been having a tough day and his scorecard had a bevy of double and triple bogies on it. His drive on eighteen was a huge slice to the right. There were cars parked on the road next to the course and somehow his drive missed them. The ball took a huge bounce off the road and ended up on the sub roof of our hotel. When heading to our room after the round, we saw the ball and could see that it was our playing partner's. He could not believe it had gone on the roof and spent time trying to find it even though the caddies said it was long gone.

After we all hit, Tina was up and hit a solid drive. It caught the ever-present mounds on the Old Course and rolled over to the right near the front of our hotel.

After the must have pictures on the famous Swilcan Bridge, we headed over to her ball. It was a perfect evening and a large group had gathered outside our hotel to enjoy outside cocktails, the late summer sunset, and to watch the action on eighteen. When we got closer to her ball, we realized Tina would be hitting her shot only about fifteen yards away from the group. There were going to be plenty of eyes on this shot!

Having this much attention is not her favorite thing, and I know she was nervous as she tried to pick the right club. To her credit, she took a deep breath, pulled out her trusty 7 wood, and hit a perfect shot that ran up onto the green and stopped about ten feet above the hole.

The shot was met with an appreciative round of applause from her gallery to the right and more applause from the gathering of people behind the 18th green. I know one thing for sure, Tina had a huge smile on her face while she made the walk up eighteen.

I wish the story ended with her beautiful approach shot.

When we arrived at the green it looked like a sure par finish for Tina. It was not a long putt, but it was a little downhill. Tina was overly cautious with the putt and her first attempt came up well short of the hole. Her second putt slid just outside the cup, and she settled for a painful three putt bogey five. Not the finish either of us was hoping for.

I have played countless rounds with my wife and never does a shot bother her after a round. This one did and I know she was thinking about it all during our post round cocktails and dinner.

I devised a plan that I thought might help her sour mood.

It was now 10:45 pm and the last groups had finished playing. There is daylight in St Andrews extremely late in the summer months. Since there was nobody on the 18th green, and there was still a flicker of sunlight, I said let's go back to the green and you can try the putt again. A delayed mulligan you could call it.

I told Tina if she could two putt this time, I would change the scorecard and give her a much-desired par on 18.

We headed back to the hotel and grabbed her putter and made the short walk over to the 18th green for her mulligan putt.

We found the spot and she tried again…same result! I said try again and she did…. same result! Right when she was about to try one more time, a wise guy from the roof deck at one of the private golf clubs to our right yelled out loudly "give up the game!" Obviously, he and his friends had been watching and no doubt may have had a cocktail or two!

We could not see who it was, but it was a hilarious line, perfectly timed, and Tina took it in good spirits.

That ended the 18th hole mulligan, and we headed back to the hotel for a nightcap. It had been a momentous day and it was fun to be out on the 18th green in the twilight trying to change history. Clearly history did not want to be changed!

Hole #11

BIRDIES FOR ALL

One of the great mysteries in golf is the surprise each new round can bring. One day golf is the greatest game ever and the next day you swear it will be the last time you ever touch a club. Even within a single round there is a battle that rages from shot to shot and from hole to hole. A good round can go bad with an unlucky bounce or a poor putting streak. Conversely, a poor round can turn positive with a couple of pars or a birdie or two.

At this point in my life, I have played many thousands of rounds of golf and never seen the kind of result I witnessed on a cool November day in 2018.

My wife Tina and I were playing a late season round of golf with my brother Mark and his wife Donna. We were playing at our home course, Plymouth Country Club in Plymouth, MA. Plymouth is nicknamed America's Hometown and the spot the Pilgrims chose to land back in 1620.

My memory of the round that day is fuzzy, and I am not sure if any of us were playing great or playing poorly. It was a late season round and it was cold, so I know we were playing quickly.

The 8th hole at Plymouth is a short gnarly little par three with distances that can vary from 100 yards to 140 yards. The challenging parts of this little monster of a hole are the two tiered green and false front. If you do not carry your shot far enough, it is rejected by the false front into sometimes a difficult lie in the rough. Hit your shot to the wrong tier of the green, and your chance at par is slim. This is especially true if the Plymouth greens are fast (like they normally are) and the pin is up front, and you are on the back tier.

On this day, the pin was on the front tier in the middle of the green. My brother hit a well struck shot, just to the right of the flag. With typical 8th hole bad luck, the shot carried just a bit too far, then spun backwards rolling off the false front and back into the rough.

I hit next and thought for sure I was going to make a hole- in- one. The ball never left the flag stick and stopped about three inches from the hole.

Tina and Donna stepped up next from 105 yards. Both hit amazing shots that had a chance to go in. Tina's stopped a little outside mine at a foot and a half and Donna's was just outside Tina's at three feet.

Here is where things got crazy.

Mark was up first, and he was chipping from below the hole and off the green in the rough. He hit the perfect chip for the 8th hole and used the slope to bring the ball back down towards the cup, and it went in for a birdie. An amazing shot! Birdie number one and by far the most difficult shot of any our group had.

My ball was in the ladies' line and close to the hole, so I tap it in for birdie number two for the group.

The pressure is suddenly mounting. No gimmes now with two players in for birdie and two others close to the hole. We all suddenly had the idea we could accomplish something special.

Tina putts next and she drains it for another birdie. Now the group has three birdies! Four birdies would be uncharted territory for any group I had ever played with.

Donna is up last, and she is no stranger to pressure birdie putts. She once made one on the second to last hole we played in Ireland on a prior trip. The hole was the 17th hole at Lahinch, and we all agreed prior to the trip that each of us needed to make a birdie in Ireland to go home.

Donna was the only one in the group without a birdie and she waited to the end of the trip to make hers. She drained the one in Ireland and she drained this last one too to make us four for four. Four players, four birdies, quite an accomplishment for our group! It was a one- and only-time event (so far) for all of us.

We took a picture on the green of where the three shots landed. Mark was off the green, so he took the picture. I wish we had all been in the picture, but I am not sure we thought we would go four for four!

Think about it, we are not a group of PGA tour players, we are club players with handicaps. I do not know what the odds are of doing this but with our handicaps thrown in, the odds would be pretty high against this happening.

How rare is this? I have played the 8th hole hundreds of times with different groups and never seen four birdies. Once in a while one birdie or two, but never four.

Compare this to all my rounds over my entire golfing life (thousands of rounds) and only one other time did any group come close. My sons Erik, Kurt, and Erik's friend

Josh and I played Bethpage Black, and on the par 3 8th hole three of the four of us made birdies.

The picture of us on the 8th green at PCC hangs in a place of honor on my office wall. I have seen eagles, birdies, and holes in one but never seen four birdies on a single hole again. It is a great memory and even more special to do it with family.

Hole #12

BALL HAWKER FOR LIFE

"One of my favorite memories is going to the golf course in the spring when the snow was melting and looking for golf balls. Even at his age, he got a kick out of that. It was his happy place."

A quote from Francis Ouimet's granddaughter Leslie Shea about Francis Ouimet in an article "Moment to Movement" which appeared in the Winter of 2021 edition of Golf Journal published by the USGA.

I have a confession to make.

I too, like the great Francis Ouimet, am a lifelong ball hawker. I had been afraid to admit this for a long time but by reading this article recently I now know I am in great company. What was good for Francis Ouimet, is certainly good enough for me. Reading about him searching for lost golf balls makes me feel much better about this hidden passion of mine.

For the uninitiated, ball hawking is the art of looking for lost balls on a golf course. Normally ball hawking is looked down upon by high-end private golf courses, but a staple at public courses.

Saying ball hawking is a hidden passion of mine may not be a secret to anyone who plays golf with me. It is certainly not a secret to friends who have visited my garage where the treasure trove of second chance golf balls is kept.

It is certainly not a secret to my wife, who puts up with my washing and cleaning the balls in our kitchen sink. Worse yet, I sort them by brand on our kitchen counter. The balls are on a paper towel when I sort them though. I try to do this process most times when she is out, so she does not see the mess it causes. For the record, I do make sure everything is cleaned up and spotless when I am finished.

It is not a secret either to my friend and long-time golf partner Roy Eaton, who loves getting free golf balls from my collection. Even with free balls though, once in a while I need to chide him about playing golf with dirty old balls. Nobody likes to see a golfer playing with dirty old balls. This is especially true when I know Roy has hundreds of clean ones sitting ready for action in his garage.

My wife and kids benefit too from free golf balls. My wife Tina will load up her bag before vacation and take my stock to protect her precious personalized PROV 1 logo balls from a watery death. My son Kurt some days fires off five-dollar golf balls like they grow on trees. Occasionally I need to remind him that the balls are worth something, even though they are lightly used. I tell him it would be nice if he at least tried to look for the balls when he jacks another one into the woods. To myself I say, "there's another one I'll find again next winter."

Francis Ouimet and I share another thing about being ball hawks. When we both started, we both needed to find golf balls to be able to play. In reading about Ouimet's early days, he would scour The Country Club across the street from his home to find lost balls, so he could practice and play with them. There was no budget in his household for golf balls.

For me, my original golf bag came with ten golf balls. Once I started to caddie and play caddie golf, my supply disappeared quickly. When we had slow days and member play was light at Wollaston Golf Club where I would caddie, we would head off to the woods to spots we knew that the caddiemaster would not be able to spot us, and we hunted for balls.

The holes on the old Wollaston Golf Club that provided the best opportunities were the 3rd, 4th, and 5th. Those holes came early in the round so the balls would be undamaged and there were ample woods to hide us during the hunts. In those days, the best players used balata balls, and you would need to be lucky to find one of them without a big cut (smile) in it.

In my college years, I needed to do golf ball hunting too. I did not have a ton of money and a couple trips into the woods at the Nichols College Golf course always proved profitable. At Nichols there were three holes that had trouble all down the left side. It was a wet area and I needed to have boots on to hunt there. My roommate went hunting once to this area and told me he saw a large snake on one of these holes. That did slow me down a little, but I still would go hunt when I needed balls.

Funny how life can sometimes repeat itself. As I spoke about in a previous story, Wollaston Golf Club moved to a new location in Milton and the course was redone to become Presidents Golf Course. I would practice at Presidents and sometimes would get tired of hitting balls. The same spots I searched as a caddie years ago, were still good hunting spots with the new course. I kept my ball supply high by visiting these spots once a month. In those days I was happy to find a Top Flite, Wilson Staff, or a Titleist DT.

The advent of the Titleist PROV 1 made ball hawking a whole new game. A single sleeve of golf balls could cost more than a lunch and a beer!

When the PRO V 1 line of golf balls was launched, I lived in Sandwich and played at Sandwich Hollows Golf Course. The practice area was right next to the tight 10th hole. After hitting all my practice balls on the range, I would scout around behind the range on the left side of the 10th hole because there were always balls lost in this spot. My son Erik had started to play at this point and in addition to me, he needed a supply of balls too.

My Dad had moved to Maine and joined the Cape Neddick Golf Course in Ogunquit. He took the family ball hawking to a whole new level. Cape Neddick had abundant amounts of brush and wet swampy areas. My Dad knew them all and at one point must have had more than 15,000 balls stored in his basement. We would stock up every time we visited and were able to find and try every brand of golf ball.

When there was a call for golf equipment for our soldiers in Iraq, my dad boxed up a few thousand balls from his collection and took them to the group collecting the golf equipment. Many ended up in driving ranges set up in the desert in Iraq to help entertain the troops in their down time.

My dad made a deal with Cape Neddick and traded thousands of excellent quality balls in exchange for passes to play free golf. It was a good deal for both parties and the balls were top quality, not the worn-out kinds of balls some ranges use these days.

If we hunt around in my dad's house and shed, I am sure there are still boxes of stored balls around. He has slowed down and is not out looking for balls anymore, so my guess is there are an abundant number of balls just waiting to be found at Cape Neddick.

Tina's dad Ted was no slouch either finding his "old goat balls" when he was a course ranger at Holly Ridge Golf Club in Sandwich, MA. We still have a box at our house with his collection. Ted was great at finding balls but once in a while was a bit too aggressive in his pursuit. According to Tina, even though he was doing a fantastic job moving people around the course, the staff asked him if he could at least let the balls stop rolling before putting them in his pocket.

As for me, I now belong to Plymouth Country Club. I have always hunted for balls during rounds played, especially if play is slow or if I am looking for a playing partner's ball. Four years ago, Tina and I started to walk the course in the winter for exercise. Tina would walk down the middle of the fairways (where she normally hit her ball) and I took a different route, down the sides of holes and a short way into the woods. The results have been spectacular, and I have averaged finding six hundred balls a winter.

For the walks, I now carry a small collapsible backpack. I quickly learned that the balls I was finding would not fit in my pockets. In golf season, I have a box in my car that holds about fifty balls. Just playing and walking I normally fill the box every few weeks. Once the box is filled, I wash, clean, and sort the balls by brand into different boxes in my garage.

I am certainly thankful for the members at Plymouth as they play high-quality golf balls. My estimate is 60% of the balls I reclaim are Titleist premium brands, PROV 1, PROV X or AVX. Callaway and Taylor Made make up 20% with various other brands making up the balance. A growing percentage are bright colors or patterned balls. Young kids love these brightly colored balls!

When I would tell people at the club the number of balls I was finding, most did not believe me. In 2022 I decided to do an actual count for the year. I ended the year at 1,788 balls found, a record year!

As Francis Ouimet found out at the beginning of this story, sometime the balls just rise up from the ground when the snow melts and the frost retreats from the ground. It is amazing to see. Even though I have found thousands of golf balls at PCC, there are always more. The grass dies, the wind blows the leaves, and if you walk slowly and look down, balls are there waiting to be found.

The interesting thing about the balls that pop up is that a few are quite old. From doing online research, I have examples of balls made back in the 1940's and 1950's. I am not sure what would happen if you hit them, but they are an interesting part of golf history.

I read an article in *Links Magazine* recently about the secondary ball industry. It is big business and the President of a company called *Foundgolfballs.com* stated his company alone sells over one hundred million recovered golf balls every year. It is an astounding number!

Friends have told me that I should join the secondary market and sell the balls I have found. I've thought about it and may give it a try. My joy comes from giving the balls away to friends, friend's children, and family. By my count I have given away over 2,800 balls. The number of balls given away will certainly grow again in 2023.

Even with all these golf balls in my garage, I do buy four dozen new balls every year. I always take advantage of the Titleist spring special and order mine with my special number (33) and some kind of little saying. I do like to have brand new golf balls to play in club tournaments. I hate losing my "special" logo balls and a few times in the winter I have found a ball I lost during the golf season. It brings me special joy to reclaim one of my own lost golf balls.

I wish I understood why I enjoy finding the lost balls so much. It could be the thrill of getting something for nothing, or the challenge of the hunt, or it could be just making the game more affordable for the people I know. Whatever it is, I know we are going to keep on walking, and I know if we do that, I will keep on finding more balls!

Hole #13

LUCKY OR GOOD?

On 11/11/21 I made a hole-in-one.

When I tell the story, without fail the first question I get is, "your first?"

My answer is my third.

This to a person is met with, "you jerk," or some other derisive comment. Not a ton of love for someone who has more than one hole-in-one.

Early on I would say five, as I have two on a local par three course. That number would draw even more ire from my golf friends. The two on the par three course did not have a witness and you need a witness for a hole-in-one, to "officially" count.

Some may say a hole-in-one is just lucky.

My favorite definition of "luck "is: Luck is when opportunity and preparedness meet. I do certainly think this applies to all the following examples but certainly a fortuitous bounce and good fortune had something to do with each hole- in- one.

The first hole-in-one I had took place at Round Hill Golf Club in Sandwich, MA. The scorecard hangs on the wall in my office and the date of the event was 8/4/88.

The round was scheduled in the late afternoon with my brother Mark and my high school friend, Joe Condon. Joe lived in Sandwich and my brother was on the Cape for a vacation.

The day turned out to be a disaster for me. This was in the times before cell phones, and I was stuck in a terrible traffic jam on Route 3 south heading to the Cape. By the time I was able to get off the highway and get to a pay phone, I was going to be at least an hour late. I called the club to let Mark and Joe know I was running way behind. They told me they would wait and said just get here when you can.

I arrived and rushed to change and get over to the tenth tee. It was getting late, and I was certainly feeling guilty about the long delay I had caused. Needless to say, the round did not start out well with a bogey on the easy par five 10th and then a double bogey on the short par 4 11th. For the record, we were playing the back nine because it was much easier to walk than the front nine. The town flipped the nines after they bought the course about a year after this round.

Up next, the short downhill par3 12th hole. It was only 120 yards, and I was hoping to turn things around and make a par.

I hit my shot and it was ugly. It was low for a wedge and hooked to the left. The shot looked like it was going to miss the green entirely. Then, the ball suddenly hit a mound near the left side of the green and went rocketing towards the hole.

The flag stick was on the right side of the green and this was good news for me. The ball shot across the green at a forty-five-degree angle and was heading at the flag at a rapid speed. Before you could blink an eye, it banged off the stick and went in the hole.

Given the inferior quality of the shot, it was amazing it went in. I would be lying if I said I was anything but stunned. I know my two playing partners were, and to this day they rib me about what a mess this shot was and how lucky I was to have it go in.

One shot certainly changed the day, and I added a chip in from the sand for a birdie two holes later. For me, what started out as a terrible round ended up being one of the first times in my life with a score under forty shots for nine holes. I made it by one shot with a solid thirty-nine.

I was excited to head into the clubhouse to buy drinks. This is the golf tradition when a person makes a hole-in-one. There were two guys sitting at the bar and it was not busy. When I announced the news to them and to the bartender, the good news was greeted with nods of indifference. I did offer to buy them a beer and they declined since the bar was closing soon.

Seeing it was late, my playing partners needed to leave too and did not have time for a drink. I went from hoping I had enough money to buy a couple drinks to not buying any.

I still get grief about this shot, but in the end, it went in and that is all that counts!

Fast forward 31 years to Plymouth Country Club. It took a long time for me to get the second one.

On this day, I had played eighteen holes in the morning in a member tournament. I had played well and was sitting with my group having a beer and lunch. My phone rang and it was my son Kurt.

Kurt and his friend Jerome MacLeod were out playing the front nine. They were on the seventh hole and called to see if I wanted to join them on the back nine. I briefly hesitated, but they convinced me to get a cart and come out and play. Jerome is a great kid and I had not seen him in a long time, so off I went to play nine more holes.

The tournament was a two-day event, and I vaguely remembered a USGA rule about playing again on a course during tournament rounds. I stopped at the pro shop to make sure I was safe to play, and our pro Mike Roy said it was fine.

I headed out to our 10th hole, a 180-yard par 3. It is a strong par three that has a large bunker to the right, a false front, and a steep drop off to the left. I needed a couple minutes to get loose, so Jerome and Kurt hit first.

After four warmup swings, I hit what looked like an exceptionally good shot at the left center of the green. The pin was in the back middle of the green and the wind was in our face, but noticeably light. Unusual for Plymouth as there always seems to be a steady breeze with the ocean so close by.

I knew the shot was good and bent over to pick up my tee. Just when I was about to grab it both Kurt and Jerome were calling for me to look up. The shot had landed right online with the pin and looked like it had a chance to go in.

I quickly looked up in time to see the shot rolling towards the hole, and a second later it went in!

It was certainly a shock and unexpected but there was no doubt the ball was in, and Kurt got his phone out and took pictures and a video of me taking the ball out of the hole. About ten seconds after the ball had gone in, the picture of me plucking the ball out of the hole was up on Instagram!

I knew right away this would be different than the one at Round Hill. It was a beautiful Saturday afternoon and there were sure to be people in the bar looking for their free drink. Luckily for me, Plymouth does have a hole-in-one insurance program.

We finished the nine holes and headed to the bar. It was late afternoon and the dinner crowd had not arrived yet, so the bar bill was reasonable.

I was happy to celebrate this time and at least a few people were around to share the good news and have a celebratory beverage!

The last ace happened on 11/11/21 at the 11th hole at the Cholla course at We-Ko-Pa resort in Fort McDowell, AZ (right next to Scottsdale). The day was Veteran's Day, and the number 11 certainly was prevalent.

This stop was to be the end of a whirlwind few days of vacation. Tina and I stayed at the Fairmont Scottsdale Princess and played TPC Scottsdale, home of the wild Waste Management Tournament on the PGA Tour. This event takes place annually on Super Bowl weekend. Then we headed for Sedona and the Grand Canyon for two days and closed our trip out with two days playing the great golf courses at We-Ko-Pa.

Since we had driven over two hundred miles before our first tee time, we decided to arrive early at We-Ko-Pa. They had a great lunch spot, right at the course and a fantastic practice area. After a long time in the car, we figured we would need a little extra time to get loose.

Just when our lunch arrived, a man came into the dining area calling out our names. We got his attention and over to our table he came. He was the course starter, and his message was simple. He let us know that there was a group of twelve guys from a bachelor party going out in front of us and he expected them to be terribly slow. He wanted to know if we could go out right away and get in front of them.

Looking at our lunches we said no thanks, but he told us to get ready as soon as we could, and he would do the best he could to squeeze us in.

Squeeze us in? So much for relaxing and enjoying the nice lunch and super practice area. We ate quickly and packed up some of the lunch and rushed off to get a couple swings in at the range.

Our friend the starter showed up after we had hit a couple balls and asked if we were ready. He had an opening now if we could head to the tee. We did, but at first it looked like there was no room for us. After he had a discussion with a group on the tee, he told us we could go ahead of them, and we were up.

We started on hole ten and you could tell right away this round was going to be longer than normal. Lots of hitting shots and waiting but the weather was perfect, and we were on vacation, so we decided to just enjoy the unique desert landscape and wildlife.

I had decided to play the combo tees that day. Every course we had played during our visit was playing longer than expected due to the recent overseeding of grass all the courses had done. Fairways were not being cut short so the new grass for the winter could grow in. The 11th hole was listed on the scorecard at 187 yards from the combo tees.

When I got up to the tee, the distance from the combo tee was much less than the 187 yards on the card. The green was large, and the pin was near the front of the green. My GPS watch said 141 yards to the front, so it looked like a shot of 144 yards to the hole.

After a brief discussion about whether I was playing the right tees, I decided with Tina's help that the combo tees where the best choice for today. It was a wise decision.

I picked an eight iron and made some practice swings. We had to wait quite a while for the group in front of us to clear the green. Waiting is not usually my strongest suit. Tina made me turn around and talk to her so I would not become aggravated with the snail like pace of play.

Finally, it was time to hit. The shot came off the club nicely and flew at the left front of the green. The sun was in our faces, and it was not easy to see, but we did see the ball bounce on the green and take a hop to the right. It looked like it was moving fast, and I expected to see it roll by the stick, but I never saw it. I assumed it must have been the tough light that blocked our vision.

When we arrived at the green, we found Tina's ball quickly but mine was nowhere in sight. Since it bounced hard, I walked thirty yards to the back of the green, but there was no ball. We looked off to the left, no ball. Tina was near the front of the green, so I asked her to check the hole just in case. We have done this a million times over the years and the ball is never in the hole.

Well, this was the one in a million. Tina excitedly exclaimed, "there is a ball in the hole, and it has your number thirty-three on it! You have yourself a hole-in-one!" I could not believe it.

We took pictures and Tina took the ball for safe keeping.

Being that this was a club where we did not know a soul, I bought two drinks after the round, one for Tina and one for me. It was a good enough celebration, and I could not see the value in spending money to buy drinks for a bunch of strangers I would never see again. Call me cheap, but I would do it the same way if it happened again.

The pro shop was great, and they gave me a special hole-in-one ball marker and a picture of the hole. I ordered a plaque to commemorate the event. I thought the plaque was part of the hole-in-one package, but it cost me a hundred dollars. I saved on the drinks and was glad to have the plaque no matter what the cost.

The round ended up well, and I managed to shoot one of my best scores ever, a three over par, seventy-five.

Although each hole-in-one was quite different, they all share an element of luck. In two of the rounds, I was incredibly lucky just to be playing and for the most recent one, I normally do not play well when I have to wait a long time to hit a shot.

The lesson learned is you just never know when the odds that the 1 in 12,500 shot is going to happen for a hole-in-one!

Hole #14

RANDOM ENCOUNTERS
OF A CELEBRITY KIND

Hang around any of the top golf courses in Massachusetts and it will not be long till you run into some kind of celebrity. Golf has certainly become a favorite pastime of many of Boston's athletes and luminaries.

A good place to start with these encounters would be our own home course Plymouth Country Club.

The Wahlberg brothers (Mark and Donnie) will sometimes make an appearance at PCC. The family owns property in the area and both Mark and Donnie love their golf and have a membership at PCC. Mark's golf backyard practice area (he sold the house in 2023) was recently featured in a Golf Magazine video, and it is unbelievable. Having Donnie show up once in a while is extremely exciting for my wife, Tina, as she is a long-time fan of his TV show Bluebloods.

Our family has seen Donnie three times and he is always very accommodating to the PCC staff and members, taking pictures and signing autographs in the bar when he comes inside. Saying that, most members give him his space and allow him to play without interruption.

Two years ago, Donnie was playing with a friend in a twosome behind us. The course was busy that day and he was buzzing around trying to find free space. He caught us on the fourth hole. We asked him if he wanted to play through, and he said no that he and is partner had found a "good place" and were happy to just stay right where they were.

The highlight of Tina's day came a short time later on the eighth hole. The eighth, that I have written about before, is a tough and short par three with little room for error. Tina hit a solid shot that stopped ten feet from the flag. It was the best shot of the group and when we approached the green all of a sudden there was applause coming from the adjacent seventh green. When we looked over, there was Donnie on the seventh green giving Tina a nice golf clap for the shot. I wish I had been closer to see the blushing red cheeks on Tina's face! It was a memorable moment, and I am sure she really wanted to run over and give Donnie a big hug.

Donnie comes to the course more often than Mark, but I have seen Mark once too. It was my second year being a member at PCC and I had come down late in the day to play a nine-hole practice round. The course was empty but when I arrived, I could see a person standing on the first tee who looked to be waiting for his playing partners. I headed over to the pro shop to see what was going on. When I checked in, our pro said it was fine to go out, but I might want to check with the guy standing on the first tee. That guy was Mark Wahlberg.

Mark was waiting for his entourage (you cannot make this stuff up) and looked irritated that they had not arrived. I said hello and asked if I could jump ahead as it looked like he was waiting for people. He said hello and said sure go ahead. All was good, but now I had to hit my shot with him watching. Thankfully, I hit a good one and got a "nice shot" from him. I moved on quickly and it was the last time I saw him that day.

Hockey players always seem to be the most congenial of the professional athletes and none better than Boston Bruins great Bobby Orr. My family and I have had numerous interactions with Orr over the years and all have been memorable

The first for me was at the post office in Forestdale, MA on Cape Cod. I was heading to check my mailbox, and I heard a gentleman chatting with the ladies at the window. When I was leaving, I came face to face with Bobby when he was carrying a handful of packages out of the post office. He was like a regular guy and thanked me for holding the door. Turns out he has a home at the private gated golf club in Sandwich MA, The Ridge Club.

The next encounter with Orr was at the taping of the Tucker Anthony Golf Classic that was first filmed at Holly Ridge Golf Course and then later moved to The Ridge Club. The event was open to the public and with one of my friends we took our children over to watch the action.

There were plenty of other celebrities at this event, but Orr was the big attraction. When they paused the filming for lunch, Orr was mobbed with picture and autograph seekers. To his credit, he stayed till every last person got their picture or autograph. It was above and beyond and near the end, the TV hosts were telling him he needed to break away from the group and eat. Time was running out for him to eat his lunch!

My sons Erik and Kurt both were caddies at the Ridge Club. Both had the pleasure of being a caddie in a match Orr played in, in the annual summer member guest. The boys told me that Orr was always kind to the kids and always waited to the end to take the youngest and least experienced caddie for the event. The boys said that Orr would make sure to get his caddie's home address and would send the lucky person a personalized autographed photo of the famous shot of him flying through the air scoring the winning goal in the 1970 Stanley Cup finals.

My last memory with Orr happened a few years ago at a charity golf event at the Pinehills in Plymouth, MA. It was a celebrity event in which each group was assigned a famous Boston sports athlete to play with. Liberty Mutual, the company I worked for, was a sponsor of the event and I had the opportunity to take a group of clients to this outing.

The day started out with heavy rain and numerous celebrities dropping out at the last minute, including the celebrity for our foursome. My group was not upset about this, and they were happy to just be playing golf. We were all standing at our golf carts talking and warming up when Orr appeared on the range. In a bit of a surreal moment, he approached us and said, "Hello guys, I am Bobby Orr, nice to meet you all." Our group response was "of course you are Bobby Orr!"

Orr then asked the group for a favor. In his rush to leave his home at the Ridge Club, he had forgotten to grab his golf clubs off his golf cart that was parked in its own garage at his home. He had asked someone from the Ridge Club to drive the clubs up for him but due to the rain, there was terrible traffic coming off Cape Cod and the clubs had not yet arrived.

Orr asked us if he could borrow clubs from us to warm up. Next thing we knew he was using our clubs and hitting balls just like one of the guys in our group. Once the warmup was over, we gathered around him for a memorable group picture.

When we arrived at the first tee Orr was there too. He realized that we were one of the groups without a celebrity and offered to stand in with us for our group's first tee team picture. Frequently during the day, he came back to our group during slower play to hang out with us to talk and have a beer. He could not have been more accommodating or gracious.

After the golf event was over, Orr hung around for lunch, and we were able to get our first tee pictures autographed by him. It was an impressive display for an athlete who had done events like this thousands of times. It certainly left a lasting impression on my guests and me that we will never forget.

My family had another great golf celebrity experience thanks to my son Kurt being a caddie in the pro-am practice round during the Deutsche Bank golf event at the TPC Boston Club. Kurt was an Ouimet Scholarship recipient like his brother Erik, and each year the Ouimet Scholars were invited to caddie for the pro-am players in this event. Groups were assigned on a first come first served basis, so Kurt had to get up at 4 am to make sure he got a loop.

After a brief bit of confusion and a false start, Kurt had his choice of a number of professional golfers. Being golf savvy, Kurt knew that Justin Rose had just won the US

Open earlier that summer and he jumped at the chance to be in Rose's group.

It was an interesting choice. A few years before, at this same tournament, we watched Rose for a long time on the putting green. He talked a lot about making putts to win the Ryder Cup but kept a safe distance from those of us around the green trying to get pictures and autographs. At least to me, he seemed self-absorbed and snobby. A good deal of time had passed since that day, so we were eager to see how Rose managed this event.

It turned out to be a smart choice and Rose and his then caddy Mark Fulcher were outstanding. There were quite a few people walking with the group inside the ropes and Rose took time to spend one hole walking with each. I know with Kurt he talked about school, tour life and much about travel. Rose told Kurt that golf had allowed him to see the entire world and he encouraged Kurt to travel as much as he could. It was great advice, and I am sure it helped Kurt with his decision to spend a semester in Ireland when he was in college.

For us being in the gallery, it was fun to get up close and hear how Rose and Fooch (his caddie's nickname) approached each shot. Their precision and pre-shot routine with each swing was amazing, like watching a rocket launch. Rose rarely missed the target that Fooch and he had picked out.

At the end of each hole Rose would patiently sign autographs for the fans who waited by the players exits. At the end of the round, Rose and Fooch both posed for pictures and signed autographs for all in the group. One of my favorite pictures from that day is Kurt posing with Fooch next to Justin Rose's golf bag. Rose and Fooch made it a great and memorable day.

Another memory from that day for Tina and me was running into Rose's long time swing coach Sean Foley on the bridge on the ninth hole. We asked him for an autograph, but he said that he did not sign them. The reason he explained was he felt that was something only the players should do. He did say he would be happy to have a picture taken and I got a good one of Foley and Tina together. Foley had a number of clients playing in the pro-am and he was running around trying to watch each of them play a couple holes.

The most lucrative celebrity encounter took place for Kurt at another Ouimet related event. It was the NFL Alumni Annual Charity Golf Event and again Kurt was a caddie. There was a bevy of old time New England Patriots and former NFL players in attendance, and Kurt was in a group captained by former Pats defensive lineman Garin Veris.

It was an interesting day for Kurt. One of the players in his group was not feeling well and asked Kurt to take over and play for him for a few holes. But the story gets better.

At the putting green, a contest was being held to attempt a $10,000 putt. Each player had to make three putts from varying lengths to qualify for the final. Since Kurt was doing some playing that day, his group had him try the putts, and he sunk all three and made the final!

There was a good-sized field for the final and a big crowd watching to increase the pressure. Somehow, Kurt drew the last spot to attempt the 50-foot putt. With a borrowed putter from one of his group, Kurt gave the putt a rap and banged it in the hole for $10,000. The place went wild, and Kurt was told it was the first time ever anyone had made the putt. All the Patriot players attending came over and signed the tablecloth at the table at which he was sitting. Kurt was told he would have his money in two weeks.

Or so we thought.

A week went by, then two, then a month, no word, and no check. Luckily, Kurt had the phone number of former Patriots punter and quarterback Tom Yewcic. Yewcic was the President of the Patriots NFL Alumni chapter. At this point and with this amount of money involved I figured it was time to help out and find the underlying cause for the delay.

I called Mr. Yewcic and after a brief bit of small talk he told me there was a slight problem with the insurance company. Working for an insurance company this statement made me nervous.

The news was bad, there was a misunderstanding in how the contest was to be administered, and only one person was supposed to get the shot at the $10,000 putt, not a large group. The insurance company had declined payment due to their discovering too many people had attempted the putt. Mr. Yewcic asked me to give him two weeks and said he would get back to me. He optimistically quipped that he had a few ideas on how to solve this problem.

Again, a week went by, then two, then three and this was looking like it was not going to be a positive outcome for Kurt.

I called Mr. Yewcic back and he apologized for the delay. He said he had been trying to negotiate with the insurance company but was not having success. He said in lieu of this news he had an idea. He said he had extra money put away for "unforeseen circumstances" and he proposed a $5,000 payment and an invite for Kurt and me to play in the NFL Alumni event the following year.

Since the event was located a long way from our home, I proposed an alternative of a $6,000 payment with no golf event invite. Mr. Yewcic agreed that this was a reasonable compromise. Given the circumstances, this seemed like a fair deal for both.

A week later, the check showed up with a nice note. Kurt used the money to fund his semester abroad in Ireland. It was a generous gesture by Mr. Yewcic and the Patriots alumni to make good on his mammoth putt.

The last celebrity encounter is my favorite because it was so unexpected.

A group of clients and I had won a regional Liberty Mutual Invitational Golf Tournament and the prize for this was an invitation to the national championship event being held at TPC Sawgrass in Ponte Verde, FL. The host of this national championship event was two-time US Open winner Curtis Strange.

Strange came to the event to do two instructional clinics for the participants and was the keynote speaker at the final night's gala banquet.

My son Erik was fortunate to receive a scholarship from the Francis Ouimet Scholarship Fund and received an additional scholarship from Ouimet from the Thomas W. Strange Endowed Scholarship. This endowed fund was dedicated to Curtis Strange's dad Thomas, who was a long-time club pro. This scholarship was created when Strange was honored by the Ouimet Fund as their "Man of the Year" in 2000.

During the cocktail hour on the last night of the event, my group and I had the opportunity to meet and talk with Curtis Strange. I let him know that our family appreciated that Erik had received this scholarship honoring his dad and it had helped with his college expenses.

Strange was intrigued by my comments and told me it was the first time he had met face to face with a family member who had benefitted from the scholarship. He then asked me for Erik's address. He told us that when he returned home and had time, he wanted to write Erik a letter.

It was a nice thought, but like many promises that are made at events like this, I wondered if anything would come of it.

Not long after the event, a handwritten letter showed up at our house with a North Carolina home return address. It was a bit of a mystery, but when Erik opened the letter, it was from Curtis Strange!

It was an impressive letter and clearly Strange had put significant effort into writing it. It was an incredibly positive message about golf and about experiences he had with his father in golf. We managed to save the letter and it survived multiple moves. It was such a wonderful thing for him to do, that a few years ago we had it framed so it would never be destroyed.

It was a unique promise to make and keep by a professional athlete and we have great admiration for Curtis Strange and how he went out of his way to do what he said he would.

We are certainly glad to have had these celebrity encounters and all of them have been memorable. We certainly understand that fame has its price and can be difficult, but from this group, it was impressive to see how all of them managed meeting and interacting with us.

Hole #15

PASSING ON THE PASSION: THE BROTHERS' MATCH

Growing the game of golf has been one of the key messages from the PGA of America, the USGA and the PGA Tour. For me, growing the game started at home, and I am fortunate that both my sons, Erik, and Kurt, have become skilled golfers. This in addition to my wife, Tina, who is an enthusiastic and skilled golfer, as well. We are a true golfing family.

Before I review the history of the Brothers' Match, a little background on both Erik and Kurt.

Erik and Kurt have taken different roads in their golf lives, but I am proud of both as they have become talented players and more importantly good people.

When Erik was able to walk, he would go with me to the driving range at Holly Ridge Golf Club in Sandwich, MA. I had cut down a five iron for him and I would buy two buckets of balls, one for him and one for me. Erik would whack away at them, and his bucket would be gone by the time I had hit ten of my balls. The balls Erik hit did not go far, so I would walk out onto the range and fill his bucket again. I would then try to hit all my balls before he finished the second bucket. Most times I was successful but once in a while I had to give him two or three of mine to keep him happy.

In 1999 there was an important event that changed Erik's golf life. The Town of Sandwich, where we lived, bought the Round Hill Country Club. I did mention this event in a previous chapter.

In those days, the Town of Sandwich was growing rapidly. The owners of the Round Hill property had the ability to build hundreds of houses around the golf course. For a town that was already growing more than it could manage, the development at Round Hill could have forced the town to build another school at a cost of at least 34 million dollars.

The town, fearing this cost, bought the property for approximately 11 million dollars and renamed the course Sandwich Hollows. The town agreed not to develop the property and would continue to run the golf course. This was the best news ever for Erik. For Christmas that year, one of his presents was a junior membership to Sandwich Hollows. The cost of the membership was a reasonable $250. Even better news for Erik was when golf season arrived, he learned that two of his good friends received the same present and wanted to play tons of golf that summer.

Erik and his friends Matt Schmidt and Mike Kinchla spent most summer days at The Hollows. The pro at the time, Micky Herron, encouraged them to play as much as they could and play in every tournament, they could fit in. The membership took them under their wing and kept an eye on them since they spent extensive time at the course. I do not think there could have been a safer place for a group of young kids to hang out. Their continuous play led to rapid improvement and soon a chance to try out for the high school golf team.

My mom and dad had a winter place in Bradenton, FL that was close to the IMG Academy. IMG is home to the David Leadbetter Golf School which Erik attended three times with the help of his grandparents and me. It was a fantastic learning experience with top level golf instruction.

The ambitious goal his friends and he set when they were freshman in high school was to win the state championship by the time, they were seniors. In 2005 they were able to accomplish this feat and won the states. Impressive that they were able to set that goal and achieve it. Certainly, the town buying Sandwich Hollows played a significant role in this achievement.

Erik has played in multiple state amateur events in MA including the Mass Amateur twice. Erik and I have played in the Mass Golf Father & Son four times and will do it again in 2023. Erik's wife Patty is a talented player too and has won the club championship at Presidents Golf Course in Quincy twice and once at Sandwich Hollows. Erik and Patty have played in multiple state level team events together and had their best finish, second, in the 2022 Mass Golf Sheeren Cup event for married couples.

Kurt took a slightly different route. He was a three-sport athlete in high school playing soccer, basketball (team captain) and baseball. Kurt played on great soccer teams at Sandwich High and in his senior year his team made it to the state semi-final game.

Kurt dealt with adversity during his senior year in sports, especially with soccer. An over aggressive parent who had the coach's ear, unfairly led to the coach taking away his starting position. It did not last long and to his credit, Kurt played hard and won his position back quickly.

In all three sports Kurt was the recipient of the team award for outstanding sportsmanship. This recognition was something we were all immensely proud of. Kurt always kept a positive outlook through some trying times.

The adversity from other sports certainly has helped in his golf development. He has maintained the same attitude of not giving up and working hard, which is needed to succeed in any sport, but especially in golf.

Kurt was always busy and did not have a ton of time for golf. Given our family though, he has developed a great swing and game. Like Erik, he went to Leadbetter for a week of quality golf instruction. Leadbetter taught him solid fundamentals which are so important in playing the game.

My brother Mark and I had a different background than my boys. We grew up in North Quincy, MA and both played football. Golf came later in life for both of us. Mark was a long-time member at Furnace Brook Golf Course and is a past President of the club. We have played together twice at my course, Plymouth Country Club, in our annual three-day member guest called the Travis.

Since we had two sets of brothers who played golf, we decided it would be fun to have a brother versus brother match every year or so. The old guys versus the young guys would be the theme.

We decided on a very inventive name for our match: *The Brothers' Match.*

The matches are played for no money stakes; but in the beginning, the losing team would have to wear hats the next year provided by the winning team. There were some beauties, with Mark finding hunting camouflage golf hats for the boys after one of our early wins. We have gotten away from this over the past few matches, but we will re-introduce this tradition in the next match.

If you were a betting person, you would put your money on the more athletic (in their minds) young guns.

It might seem that the young guys would have been the better bet, but most of the matches have been close. Frequently, they have been decided by the last putt on the last hole. This was the case at Blue Hill Country Club for the first match we ever played. The shortish par 5 18th hole at Blue Hills provided good drama for the first win by the old guys with Mark making a clutch putt to seal the victory.

The next year the match was played at the Waverly Oaks Golf Course in Plymouth, MA. The match was decided by a clutch par and a "grip it and rip it" drive by Kurt which led to the only draw of the Brothers' Match. Kurt made a clutch putt on the 18th green to secure the tie.

The match moved to Mark's long time home club, Furnace Brook Golf Club, and the first of two blowout wins for the young guns took place. Erik was on fire and was close to even par, and the old guys had no answer that day.

The old guys used this drubbing as motivation and went on a three-match winning streak. Matches took place at Old Barnstable (my home course for four years), Wollaston Golf Club (where both Erik and Kurt worked then) and lastly at my now home course Plymouth Country Club. All three matches were close, and the old guys needed to make short putts on the 18th hole in a couple of the matches to secure the wins.

The young guys turned things around and have now gone on a three-match winning streak. A tight match at Plymouth, followed by a close match at a neutral site, the beautiful Donald Ross designed Winchester Country Club. The Winchester match came down to the last putt. Poor putting by me on 17 and 18 and strong play by Erik on those holes helped the young guys to a victory.

The last time we played the match was again at Plymouth Country Club. Now both Kurt's and my home course. The young guys brought their A games and put a big time beating on the old guys. Given the history, this says the old guys should be ready and motivated for the next match.

After nine matches the count stands at four wins for the old guys, four wins for the young guys and one draw. The matches have been slowed a bit by Covid over the past two years, but I have no doubt we will play the match again in 2023.

We have established an enjoyable tradition with the Brothers' Match. The competition is what it should be in golf, fierce but friendly. We play for bragging rights and who gets to pick the hats for the next match. Both sides play hard and then we enjoy food, beverages, cigars (all but me on the cigars) and re-living the round when the playing is done. It is like a much smaller version of the Ryder Cup when the pros play for no money and possession of a trophy. Kind of the way things should be more often and to me what the game is all about: Passion and Tradition!

Hole #16

CHASING MAJORS AND THE SPECTATOR GRAND SLAM

Shortly after I started playing frequent rounds of golf, I wanted to find a way to watch the professional golfers on the PGA Tour play in person. We were lucky, in New England we had a PGA golf tournament at Pleasant Valley Country Club in Sutton, MA. This event had various sponsors over the years and was held at the same location from 1965 through 1998.

I was fortunate to attend this event three times and it was amazing to see how far the pros hit the ball and how they could control the balata ball with persimmon woods. There was only one thing lacking at PV, the big names of golf. Due to the fall date, many of the top ranked professionals would not play at Pleasant Valley unless the PGA Tour mandated it, due to the event being held late in the PGA tour year.

As I played more, I wanted to see the top players, and I figured out that the only way to do this would be to attend a major. In 1984 the US Open was going to be played at Winged Foot Golf Club in Mamaroneck, NY. I took a look at a map and determined that it would be a three hour drive down route 95 to get to the club. Since I enjoyed driving and already did a considerable amount of it for work, I decided that I would buy a weekday ticket and drive to the course to attend. My logic was I wanted to attend the event before the cut in case any of the top players did not make it to the weekend.

The process of buying the ticket showed how far things have come in golf and with the US Open. I read an advertisement in one of the golf magazines about how to buy tickets for the event. I called Winged Foot and spoke with someone at the club. They asked what day I wanted to attend and then told me to send a $15 check to the club and they would send me back a ticket.

A week later the ticket arrived at my home. It was an uncomplicated process and a very reasonable price to see the best golfers in the world.

The day came and the ride down was smooth, and I made it in the planned time of three hours. The directions to the club were well marked and I rolled in and parked on the Winged Foot East Course that was not being used for the US Open and was turned into a large on-site parking lot. I remember looking at the fairways and thinking these fairways look like the greens I putt on at the public course I play.

I was able to follow the day's golfing greats like Jack Nicklaus, Greg Norman, Lee Trevino, and Seve Ballesteros. This Open was the first one that Arnold Palmer had not qualified for in thirty-one years, and it made me sad that I would not see him. My son Erik and I did get to see the King a few years later when he played in the US Senior Open at Salem Country Club in Peabody, MA. We both remember watching him play the second and third holes at Salem followed by a large gallery of "Arnie's Army."

The moment I remember most from my first US Open took place when I was heading out on the course to find a new hot shot young player. Freddie (Boom, Boom) Couples was playing, and I had read about his immense length off the tee. As I approached a tee with few people around, I heard a pop that sounded like a rifle shot. It was Freddy hitting a mammoth drive off the tee. Even with all the top players in the world at the event, the sound he made when he hit his driver was different from the rest of the players. It was striking to hear it.

The ride home was long when thunderstorms came through late in the afternoon, and I was fortunate to get out of the parking lot just before the rain started. There was one small road in and out of the golf course. On Sunday of the tournament the traffic was so snarled trying to get into the club that the golfers with the later tee times had to get out of their cars and walk to the course. I was glad I went early on a weekday after hearing about all the Sunday traffic issues.

Going to this event got me hooked on going to the Majors and the calendar was lining up well to do it again as the US Open was going to be held on the East Coast again. It would be at Shinnecock Hills on Long Island in 1986 and then coming to The Country Club in Brookline, MA in 1988.

Things did change with the tickets when the event grew bigger in 1986. This time there was no calling the club for tickets. Now, the USGA managed the ticket distribution, and a lottery was set up due to high demand. I was lucky to get a ticket to Shinnecock, due to the ticket sales being limited to 25,000 people per day.

There is always luck involved in picking the day to attend, and 1986 was no different. I drove down to stay with a relative in New York City on Thursday in a driving rain. The pictures from the Thursday round were striking. High winds, rain, and high scores. When I arrived and parked my car on Friday it was a beautiful day with clear blue skies, and I was thankful to have picked the right day.

My memory of this Open was predictions of hideous traffic that would cause issues getting to the course. I left the city early in the morning and had no issues at all with traffic or parking.

The setting and course were beautiful and the clubhouse sitting on top of a hill near the 9th and 18th greens was iconic in how it sat stately above the links. Purists may debate if Shinnecock is a "true" links as it is not right on the water, but it looked like a links course to me.

I wish I had more vivid memories of the round, but again I was amazed by the length and accuracy of the golfers at this event. The course was tough and tight with high rough, but beautiful. Certainly, eye opening for me, seeing that I had never been to this part of the country. Years later I would get the chance to return with my son Erik. But more on that later.

Two years later the Open would return to the Country Club in Brookline, MA and there was a frenzy in the Boston area to get tickets. The US Open was now an event that everyone wanted to attend.

There was a lottery to obtain tickets, and I was not successful. Fortunately, a friend I worked and played golf with back in those days won tickets in the lottery. He was kind enough to invite me to go along with him. I was amazed at how much the event had grown in just four years.

It turned into an interesting and perfect day to watch golf. This time, we attended on Thursday. It would be the first time for me on the grounds of this famous club and given how close it is to the city, I was looking forward to seeing what it looked like.

While we were walking along following Greg Norman, we were surprised to see Boston Celtics star Larry Bird following Norman along with us with a large crowd. Bird lived close to the course and if he wanted to, I bet could have walked over from his house nearby. Our timing with finding this group was fortuitous. Norman had pushed his drive to the right into a rocky ledge area. He hurt his wrist when he hit a buried rock on his next swing. My lasting image from Norman that day was his sitting in a cart with the arm in a sling, doing interviews with the press near the clubhouse. It seemed a fitting ending for a guy who had frequent crash and burn finishes to major tournament rounds.

After being there in person, it was fun to watch it on TV and see Curtis Strange get up and down from a bunker in front of the 18th green to force a Monday playoff with Nick Faldo. If I did not have to work, I might have tried to go over and see the playoff that was won by Strange.

The major chase went on hold after a nifty run. Having kids and far away locations for the US Open made it tough to get out to see any more.

As luck would have it, the 1999 Ryder Cup was coming to The Country Club. The long-time sleepy matches had become more competitive in recent years and the European team now had the majority of the top players in the world. Although not officially a major, it had become more important to players on both sides and had major championship like tension and passion for both players and fans. It was a hot ticket in Boston in 1999.

The company I worked for at the time, CNA Insurance, bought a package with multiple passes each day and a tent across the street with food and beverages. The package we purchased came with a pro-am event that was held at another area course. The company decided to fly our best clients in from all around the country to play in the pro-am and attend the matches.

To save money, our local office rented large twelve passenger vans and a group of employees, including me, made stops at Logan Airport, The Royal Sonesta Hotel in Cambridge, and then went over to the Country Club to drop off guests at the practice rounds. I became a van driver for two days and had a blast. I was able to meet our best clients from all over the country.

The reward for my driving was two practice round tickets and a ticket to the Saturday matches. I was more than happy to trade this taxi work for tickets.

This Ryder Cup took place in the infancy of the Tiger Woods craze and the crowds and ticket demands were unprecedented. Unlike the 1988 Open where we parked next door at the Lars Anderson Museum, for this event spectators were encouraged to take public transportation.

The round on Saturday was one of the best golf events I have attended. I decided to follow a match between David Duval and Davis Love, versus young Spanish star Sergio Garcia and veteran Swede Jasper Parnevik. It was a back-and-forth affair that came down to the last hole and ended in a half (tie). The normally stoic Duval delighted the gallery that day with his emotion and fist pumps. Love's college friend Michael Jordan was inside the ropes that day high fiving with the crowd when the Americans made long putts to win holes.

I missed the magic of the final day's singles matches and the huge USA comeback, but it was a thrill to actually get to the Ryder Cup and see what was, for me, a once in a lifetime golf event.

Speaking of once in a lifetime, certainly the toughest ticket in golf is the Masters. Thanks to my brother Mark winning the ticket lottery, my son Erik, my Dad, Mark, and I got to see Augusta National and a practice round in 2006.

Sometimes you just need good luck, and we had it that day at Augusta. When we were walking up the 11th hole heading to the clubhouse area, we ran right into Tiger Woods who had just gone off the 10th tee and was only playing the back nine this day. Everyone wanted to see Tiger play and soon the word would be out that he was on the course. We got up close to him for two holes since the gallery had not grown to the normal Tiger crowd of crazies yet.

There are so many fascinating things about walking that course but until you see it and walk it, it is hard to believe how hilly it is. You certainly must be fit as a player, caddie, or spectator to get around Augusta National. We all had tired legs that night when we returned to our hotel.

The US Open returned to Shinnecock Hills in 2004, and so did I with my son Erik who was now playing an extensive schedule of competitive junior golf. This trip turned into quite an adventure, as we decided to take the ferry across to Long Island from New London, CT. We were not the only ones taking this route and you could tell there were a sizable number of golf fans on the ferry with us.

This Open was noted for two things. The first was one of the par three greens being so fast it needed to be watered during the final round during play. The second was another Phil Mickelson near miss finish in a US Open. We arrived just in time to see the water applied, and we followed Phil for the back nine until he hit his shot on the par 3 17th in a bunker and failed to get up and down for par.

Retief Goosen was the winner, and we remember watching him on the practice putting green making everything he looked at. It was exciting to be there on a Sunday and feel the crowd's energy pulling for Phil.

The real adventure started on the drive home. By the time we made our way to the bus and offsite parking lot, it was clear to me there was no way we would make the last ferry back to New London in time. We had been sucked into watching the Phil show and went over the time it would take to make the last ferry. This was a huge mistake.

Now we would have to circle all the way back towards New York City, and it was going to be a long way home. We should have stopped but I had a golf tournament the next day and Erik had school. It was one of the longest drives of my life, and to stay awake, towards the end I was stopping every fifteen miles. Never was I so happy to get out of the car and arrive home safely.

2007 was the year I met my wife, Tina, and she had the experience of a lifetime at the 2007 PGA Championship.

Tina had the thrill of attending the PGA at Southern Hills with her brother Ted. Ted was the head golf professional at Morris County Golf Club and was involved with the PGA of America and the championship committee. Tina was able to get right up close to the action on the first tee when Ted was announcing the groups starting their rounds. She was privileged to be present inside the clubhouse for the private presentation of the Wannamaker Trophy to the winner, Tiger Woods.

Then came 2009. It must have been our year for good luck. After trying for years, we won tickets to the Masters practice round. We turned this into a longer trip and visited with Tina's brother Brian and his wife Amy in Greenville, SC. Brian and Amy attended the Masters with us, and we drove over on Wednesday morning to attend the practice round. We were up quite early, and it was a long ride down the backroads to make our way over to Augusta from Greenville.

Our arrival could not have been better timed; when we were crossing the first fairway one of Tina's favorites was playing hole number one. When I saw the pictures from that day, it was clear Tina was obsessed with Fred Couples. She took at least twenty pictures of him walking down the first fairway. I thought that we may have been spending the entire day watching Freddy! Good thing our plan was to see all eighteen holes, otherwise I would not have been successful getting Tina to move on. We did manage to walk and see the entire course and watched the par three contest.

There is no doubt that the Masters is the best run sporting event in America. Free parking, easy access to shipping items home, immaculate grounds, real bathrooms and reasonable food and drink prices are just some of the things they do right. Our lunch this day for the two of us was two pimento cheese sandwiches, two beers and M&Ms for dessert. It was just over $20! The Masters knows how to treat their "patrons" right.

When we were on our way to leave the course, we paused at the grandstands by the 13th green. The committee was working on pin placements, and they were simulating multiple angles and paths that balls would be hit on approach shots. It was quiet and peaceful, and it was fascinating to watch the care and precision they used to set the pin placements for the tournament. We sat and watched them for about an hour and admired the work they were doing.

The good luck and good timing extended to the US Open at Bethpage Black in 2009. Tina, Kurt, Erik, and I traveled down Thursday night in a driving rainstorm. One of our friends who went on Thursday, got soaked right away when he and his son arrived during monsoon like downpours.

Seeing the prior day's rain, we brought boots with us to wear to the golf course. Good thing because the mud was deep in spots. Tina was "Teenzee Tough" all-day trudging around on what is one of the toughest walks in golf.

The highlight of the day was running into Tiger on the 16th tee. We raced two holes ahead of him so we would have a good vantage point to see his tee shot. Without warning us, Kurt let out a loud "get in the hole" right after Tiger bombed one away. His timing was perfect, right after Tiger hit the ball.

It was interesting to compare how this event was run after going to the Masters. Parking was not free and the line to get lunch was 45 minutes. Once we ordered, the bill for the four sandwiches and sodas was $80. It made us appreciate the Masters even more after attending these events back-to-back.

We reached an interesting crossroads at this point. Tina had now been to three of the four majors, and I had attended two. We wondered if we could find a way to get to all four and achieve our Spectator Grand Slam of Golf. We decided to devise a plan to get to the toughest one, the Open Championship, in either Scotland or England.

Looking at the calendar, 2013 looked like the year to make it all work. The Open was going to take place at Muirfield, and St Andrews was not that far away by car or train. Thus began the plan for our adventure to Scotland to play golf and see The Open.

My brother Mark and his wife Donna were scheduled to join us on the trip. However, the trip got off to a rough start when my brother Mark was diagnosed with a detached retina, just days before we were scheduled to depart. The doctor told him he was going to need surgery immediately, and it was a good thing he had not tried to go through with the trip and fly. The flying could have resulted in more damage to his eye.

At this point it was too late for us to cancel so Tina and I forged on but with heavy hearts over what had happened to Mark.

Our travels to Scotland took place during an unusual heat wave, and the temperatures each day soared into the 80's. The heat left the courses looking brown but playing hard and fast. We had a wonderful week playing and needed to apply sun screen each day.

We decided to take the train over to Muirfield and this would require a change in Edinburgh. It seemed a safer option than driving, and even with long lines, the trains ran often and on time. It was a stress-free trip over to the Open.

We did a combo of walking to see the course and finding seats in the grandstands to watch the top groups come through. We saw Phil Mickelson make a great up and down with a flop shot for par off a rock-hard lie. This was an omen of things to come since Phil went on to win his first and only Open title.

There was a huge TV screen showing the action in the center of the course with a food court all around it. It was a good place for us to catch a little rest and nourishment.

Like clockwork, the highlight of the day was us running into Tina's favorite player, this time on a par three hole. We got close and saw Fred Couples put his chewing gum in the barrel. Tina nudged me and motioned that I should dive in and get it for her. We had a good laugh about it and an enjoyable day seeing one of the top courses in the world.

We headed back to St Andrews and the next morning drove from St Andrews to Edinburgh. It was Sunday morning and we decided to find a pub to watch the final round of The Open. It was a unique experience as the BBC covers the event differently than American TV. We saw little of Phil until the very end at the trophy ceremony. It was disappointing, because the European players were the focus of the BBC coverage, and you would have never known Phil was making a charge to win.

In preparing for our trip over to The Open we realized we could place a wager on the outcome. Tina had bragging rights on this because she picked Phil to win and cashed a sweet winning ticket. It was a wonderful way to end our stay in Scotland.

Tina now had the Spectator's Grand Slam, and I was one major short. I needed the PGA Championship to complete my slam. The PGA was not an easy one because it was not on the east coast often, but we saw an opportunity coming in 2016 when the PGA would be played in New Jersey at Baltusrol Golf Club.

With the event being held in metro New York we knew this would be a tough ticket, but we got in early and got both our tickets and hotel. Our hotel, near the Newark Airport, was recommended by the PGA. It was a dump and we complained after the event about their name being involved with a place that was of inferior quality.

The golf was entertaining, and we got to see a friend that Erik went to college with play in the event. Unlike prior events where we battled traffic and high parking prices, we decided to take an Uber back and forth to the event. All and all, the Uber worked smoothly.

This brings us full circle to 2022. Through a miracle, I was on my computer at the right time when I received an email inviting me to buy tickets for Thursday's US Open round at The Country Club. I thought the invite was a swindle and called the USGA to make sure it was legit. They told me it was, so we bought the four tickets we were allowed for $150 a ticket. A long way from the $15 a ticket from the 1984 Open! We had a blast attending, but it is certainly amazing to see how the game and these events have grown over the years.

Hole #17

YOU'RE BUILDING A WHAT?

Three years ago, I built my own backyard practice area. I'm quite sure there were people, including my neighbors and my lovely wife, who thought I had lost my mind.

Everyone should have a practice area like this. I love my little slice of paradise in my backyard, and I did all the design and construction myself. Hard to believe from a guy who is jokingly called "Mr. Fix It." Never met a nail that I could drive in straight or a household problem I could fix easily!

Saying that about my skill level, building my practice area just required digging, cutting down a few random small trees and moving material in a wheelbarrow. Even with my limited skills, I believed I could manage this project.

Jim Nance (CBS multi-sport announcer extraordinaire) has posted video of his Pebble Beach backyard with his lavish reproduction of the seventh hole at the Pebble Beach Golf Links. It is quite something and Nance made sure to make it to scale of the real seventh hole. Mark Wahlberg had a beautiful practice area too located in his backyard at his Hollywood mansion (which he recently sold). Both these have something in common that I did not have in building mine, an unlimited money supply. Mine was being built on a shoestring budget.

The thought to build my practice area started to percolate in my mind when we first bought our home. Our backyard sloped away from the house in a gradual hill. I thought right away the land was set up perfectly to build a practice bunker area in the far-left hand corner of the yard.

There were other things to do, and the project was put on the back burner. Every time I walked out to the backyard, I would look at this area and think about what fun it would be to be able to practice at home.

Seven years went by, and the thought never left me. What really got the project going was my son Kurt buying me a golf practice net. The net was large and when I tried to set it up near my garage it did not fit the space well. I went back to the area where I thought the sand trap would fit and developed a plan. There was much more room in this part of the property and this area looked like a perfect fit for my practice spot.

The area was back in the woods and a safe distance from my house. I decided if I did things right, the net and the sand trap could all fit perfectly in the same area. When I looked at the site closer, it seemed like I would have enough room for a short game chipping area too. The backyard is about eighty yards across, and my thought was it would be convenient to be able to hone my chipping game at home.

With a minimum of tree cutting and pruning, this spot would provide a shady area to have the whole practice area. The huge pine trees in our back yard would provide ample cover and make it so we would always be hitting balls from the shade.

The sand trap was the first part of the project I decided to attack. The internet provided plans on how to construct the trap and what materials I would need. I bought two new shovels to do the digging. That may have been my first mistake in this adventure.

The soil here in Hanover, MA is not friendly. Our neighboring town is called Rockland and it would have been a perfect name for Hanover too. The soil was filled with rocks of all sizes and roots, big roots from the tall trees all around our yard. My two sons said, "why not hire a bobcat?" This was a low budget affair, so the bobcat was not an option.

The digging was stop and go and difficult. I would get a couple shovels full of dirt out and then hit a huge boulder. I would try a different direction and run into a vein of thick roots or more rocks. The going was slow, and my hands and wrists took a beating from banging the shovel into the unfriendly soil. No wonder there were few farms in our town!

Although the digging was taking twice as long as I planned, the sand trap was shaping up well and it was going to fit naturally into the topography of the yard. It reminded me of the type of bunker you would find on courses designed by the popular golf architects Bill Coore and Ben Crenshaw. I have played eight of their layouts and their sand traps look natural, like they had always been there. My trap looked like this, and it looked like it belonged right in the place I had built it. Two weeks of digging was finally at an end. My hands and wrists were grateful.

Those rocks I kept hitting and digging up came in handy. The next step in the process was to build a narrow drainage trench through the bottom of the bunker. There was no need to buy any stone for this part of the project. I had just dug up close to a ton of stone and I took pleasure placing those stones in the trench and then burying them.

To prevent weeds from growing through the bottom of the trap, I laid down pliable landscape paper (it was more like plastic) and did my best to keep it smooth. I was getting close to making it look like an authentic sand trap and it was now time to order sand to fill it.

I took a ride down to our local landscape material provider and they had two grades of sand. I told the busy man behind the counter what I was doing and got a funny look. He told me this was a first for him, but he recommended a fine grain sand that was used in the base of swimming pools. They had tons of sand and if I wanted it right away, they could deliver it the next day. This sounded great, and I just asked them to drop the sand off next to my driveway near our basketball hoop.

When I arrived home that day, I was happy to see that the sand had been delivered, but my directions must have been lost somehow. The four yards of sand were dumped right smack in the middle of my driveway.

This certainly expedited the process of moving the sand because it was in Tina's parking space, and she would not be happy with the placement of it. Rapidly, I moved the sand off the driveway and out of Tina's parking space. Next, I carted the sand into the bunker that was about one hundred yards away from the driveway. As part of the project, I had just purchased a much larger wheelbarrow and I started the process of filling the sand trap. Needless to say, it took multiple trips back and forth to accomplish this task.

It was easier digging the sand than the rocky Hanover soil, and soon the trap was actually starting to look like a functional sand trap!

Once I built up a solid base, I decided to hit some balls to evaluate the quality of the sand. It worked well, and the sand felt remarkably close to the consistency of the sand at my own club. Part one of the mission accomplished.

Now I realized I needed accoutrements for my new creation. Father's Day was coming soon, and I needed a real golf rake for the trap. Tina told me to be patient as she was thinking ahead and had it covered. She was able to secure a rake from our golf pro since they had extras at the club. The rake was my most unique Father's Day present ever.

I realized I needed targets to hit at, so I looked online for a golf supplier and ordered three flag sticks. I had flags already, so this would make perfect use of them. I had to order the cups that hold the flags up too, and again had to dig into the unforgiving Hanover soil. Like anything, it took me twice as long to dig the holes for the cups as I thought it would.

With the sand trap looking good, it was time to move on to the next step. The area behind the trap was bigger than I expected and there was more than enough room for the practice net and to set up a chipping area. I decided to try my hand at growing and maintaining grass and headed to Home Depot to buy sod for my chipping area.

On paper, this seemed like a great idea and after some prep work and minor grading I rolled in the beautiful green sod.

It was beautiful for about three weeks.

I tried to hit balls off of it, but I could not keep the sod short enough to be like fairway or even rough. It was pretty to look at but not functional to hit balls off and every time I took a divot, it looked worse. The sod was in the shade and in three weeks started looking yellow. By week four it was splotchy, and this part of the experiment was not going to work out. I gave up on the grass and purchased a synthetic practice matt to hit off. It was worth a try to grow the grass, though, and for a brief time it really looked nice.

Back to site prep and after cutting down more small trees my practice net now had a lovely home at the very back of the area. In the spring when the leaves bloom it is a serene place to hit balls. Well, except when our next-door neighbor's dog roams his backyard and howls every time, I head to the practice area. Luckily, they normally quiet him down quickly but it is a bone curdling howl that always scares me.

The most important reason for building the bunker was that despite being a skilled player, Tina has always struggled to get out of sand traps. I was hoping, with a little practice at home, we could make her a more confident bunker player. We even named the trap, "The Teenzee Trap" in her honor.

Last year Tina decided she was going to get over her fear of the sand. She spent time practicing her sand shots this past spring in our yard, and 2022 was her best year ever getting out of the sand!

There is no doubt that the practice area has helped my short game and bunker game. I love going out and practicing various shots that fly at different trajectories. Having the net allows me to take full swings too. During my working days, it was a place I would retreat to for a fifteen-minute break to refresh my attitude. So far, no windows have been broken, but I have hit a few mis-directed balls that have bounced off our outdoor shower stall. Thankfully, it is made of wood and hard to damage.

During the beginning of the pandemic, before golf courses were allowed to open, my practice area was my only source for golf. I was out there multiple times a day hitting balls. It was my sanctuary!

At work, we were using an application called Brain-shark to communicate with our clients since we could not visit with them in person. To have fun, I did a video of the practice area and sent it to my work golf friends. I posted the video on LinkedIn, and it received over 10,000 views. It was fun to see the wide exposure the one little video got. I received impressive feedback and quite a few people found my comment in the video about how the signs around the bunker "had just fallen into my golf bag" comical. That quote struck a chord and led to many laughs.

The total cost of everything to do the project was $850, with the driving range matts being the most expensive part by far. Since I first did the project, I have upgraded one of the matts to one that simulates long grass like rough. It is more realistic to hit off and has a nice soft feel. As I travel around, I find innovative ideas too, like stands I made out of branches to hold the golf clubs and a fancy box my dad made to store the golf balls and lean my golf equipment against.

My friend Tom Donovan designed a logo and gave the practice area a name, "The PAR Club." He suggested that I use the logo and have shirts made and sell them. I have not gone through with that idea yet, but I like the logo and will follow through on his idea. This year, I have added a real golf ball washer like they have on all golf courses to my practice area. The more I think about it, the more ideas I seem to produce for my sanctuary!

Given the cost, having the practice area has paid me back multiple times. I certainly love thinking about more ideas to make it better!

Hole #18

HOME IS WHERE THE HEART IS BUT YOU NEED TO PLAY THESE TWO SPECIAL PLACES!

After years of searching, I am happy to have found what I know is an exceptional home golf club in Plymouth Country Club in America's Hometown of Plymouth, MA. It has been a long journey with quite a few stops, but I would not trade the journey for anything.

My first home club was Presidents Golf Course in Quincy, MA. It was the first place that I had an official handicap and I have written about it in prior stories. I would play at Presidents on weekends with friends and sneak on through the holes in the fence during the week to practice on the abandoned second green. The reason this green was abandoned was that too many golf balls flew out onto nearby West Squantum Street and into neighbors' yards, breaking their windows. Due to this problem, the hole was shortened and moved to its current location aiming away from the street.

The original second green was a suitable place for short game practice and once I would see a lull in play and an opening, I would jump on and play a loop of holes that would bring me back to the hole in the fence where I started.

I needed to find a new course once I built a house in the lovely town of Sandwich on Cape Cod. During the construction of the house, I traveled around and played all of the local courses. My favorite was Cape Cod Country Club in Falmouth MA. I always loved the course, and I needed a place to move my handicap, so Cape Cod CC was the choice.

While I loved the course and would play it with my group of friends, I would never say I felt like I was a true "member." In those days, the course did not offer full playing memberships, but there were locals who were more "regulars" than my group of friends and me.

We found this out when we played in one of the big events at the club. Every year, Cape Cod CC hosted the regional Oldsmobile Scramble qualifier. One year our team ended up in a tie for first place and participated in a sudden death playoff against a group of "regulars." It was clear that we were the outsiders and all the people watching were rooting against us. Our opponents made a birdie putt on the first playoff hole and there was no doubt everyone but us was happy with the result.

As mentioned in a prior story, the Town of Sandwich had bought Round Hill Country Club and it was time for me to move my handicap closer to home and become a member of this course. The course was re-named Sandwich Hollows, and my son Erik was a member too. Memberships for town residents were very reasonable.

My time being a member at Sandwich Hollows was not a period when I was playing my best golf and I played alone in the evening to improve. I did play in a small number of the club's tournaments, but my play was poor, and it was embarrassing. The back nine at the Hollows is tough to love too, especially when you are not hitting it well. It is too bad the original owner (who was a road builder) fired his architect as the owner felt he was too costly. He attempted to build the back nine himself and made a mess of it. While I always enjoyed playing the front nine, the back nine was never pleasant to play.

With the changing landscape of golf, towns on the Cape were opening up their courses to out of town membership. When the chance came to move over and join Old Barnstable Fairgrounds Golf Course, I jumped at the opportunity. Old Barny is one of my favorite public courses on Cape Cod. Tina loved it because it is very "women friendly" with tees that gave her a fair chance to make a good score on every hole.

While I loved the course and played it often on weeknights, I found it hard to make connections and find a regular group to play with. There was a weekday men's group, but I was still working and could not play in it. There were small groups that played together frequently, but I found it hard to break into groups like this.

Saying that, Tina and I played weekends at Old Barnstable and occasionally partnered up with some friends or clients of mine who spent time on the Cape during the summer. We loved playing the course and still go back once a year to play it.

When I moved from Sandwich to Hanover, I could not make the trek to Old Barney work. With the move we decided to give Harmon Golf in nearby Rockland, MA a try and it became my new home course. At least for a brief time.

Harmon had a large range, a short game practice area, and a short nine-hole par three course that I loved to play. We tried the "championship course" and I knew it was not going to be a long-term solution after the first round. Tina never loses balls but lost six in the one round she played there with me. She was not in a rush to go back, and I was not a huge fan of the course either.

On the good news side, Tina made a hole- in- one on the short course at Harmon from about one hundred yards on the second hole.

Once we played the six lost ball round, we decided we needed to find a workable alternative that we both would enjoy playing. We heard that Plymouth Country Club was looking to attract new members and had an economical fall membership program. I thought it might be too early to join since Kurt was still in college, but Tina thought otherwise and encouraged me to explore what the options for membership looked like.

To be sure we were on the right track I invited my good friend and longtime Salem Country Club member, Steve Roy, down to a member guest event to see what he thought about the place. His answer was an easy one, "just do it and join," he said enthusiastically. I have thanked him for his wise advice multiple times.

What made Plymouth a good fit and the right club to join? First off, Plymouth CC is an underrated golf course that is truly a Donald Ross gem. It is a par sixty-nine with only one par five, but it plays much longer than it looks. To go with this, we have a top-notch head pro and greenskeeper, who both do all they can to keep the course in amazing shape.

To me though, the key to the experience at PCC being great is the availability of group play. At PCC you can show up every day of the week, put down a couple of dollars, and get paired up to play in a game. There are net and gross games, higher handicap, and low handicap games. These games go on every day of the week and weekends too. It makes it easy to meet people and find people to play with, even if you do not know a single person when you join.

PCC does not have the amenities that other clubs have; no pool, tennis courts or large driving range, but it has a great and playable course and a membership that is easy to assimilate with. Perfect for my family and me.

Finding a home club has been awesome, but even though home is where the heart is, traveling for golf is one of our favorite pastimes. There are two places every golfer should make a pilgrimage to at least once in their lifetime. One is the greatest golf town in the world, St. Andrews in Scotland. The other is Bandon Dunes in Bandon, OR. Bandon has the best group of golf courses in one place anywhere in the world.

This is not to say that there are no other great golf destinations: Pinehurst, Hilton Head, Pebble Beach to name three. The Southwest of Ireland, the East Lothian area of Scotland are wonderful too.

I just have a soft spot for St Andrews and Bandon Dunes and feel they are the best.

What makes them so special? With St Andrews it is the combination of the town and all the great golf courses that are close by. Twenty-one in total are within a half hour drive. If you wanted, you would never have to drive and could just play the courses that the Links Trust operates in

St Andrews. You can walk to all of them from most places in town.

The town is old and just oozes the spirit of golf. There are a multitude of pubs and restaurants that can easily be walked to, and the Ladies Putting Course is a must if you want to challenge your flat stick skill. There is an abundance of historical sites and St Andrews University to visit in non-golfing hours.

Being there in the summer, when golf is still being played at 10:00 pm at night, is a unique experience. I know when we last traveled there, there was a certain sadness when it came time for us to depart. We would love to return, and I know we would never be bored with all the opportunities St Andrews offers.

Bandon on the other hand is the ultimate golfing resort experience. Some say it is too difficult to get to and others say it is in the middle of nowhere, but those things make it special.

The golf courses are the story here and they are the best collection of courses in one place that I have ever been. All unique, all playable and I have never had so much fun playing golf, even in the pouring rain on our first day at Old MacDonald.

While I loved all the courses and enjoyed playing them, I thought Bandon Trails was the most underrated. The routing is scenic, and the holes just feel so "big," as the scenery around the golf course is larger than life. This course does have the awe-inspiring spot were Bandon owner Mike Keiser stood up on a high plateau and was able to gaze out over the beautiful property. According to the plaque at this spot, it was this view that convinced Mr. Keiser that this was the place to build his dream golf resort.

The par 3 Bandon Preserve Course and the challenging Punchbowl putting green offer great entertainment and should not be missed. We had a great battle on the Punchbowl with all twelve guys from our trip going around in a spirited competition. The central driving range is massive and has Shortie's par 3 course that opens most days later in the day and is free.

The service level at Bandon was above and beyond. From the greeting by their original employee and Director of Outside Happiness, Bob "Shoe" Gasper, to the van drivers, to the starters, caddies and wait staff, they all went out of their way to provide the best experience. We never waited more than a few minutes for the van service and once you are on the property there is no need for a car.

There is no doubt both are expensive vacations, but to get the best sometimes you have to pay a little more. I believe both locations provide terrific value and experiences for the money spent. To me, one of the biggest tests of any resort is the question, would you return? In both cases the answer would be an enthusiastic yes!

Playing different venues makes me happy to come home to Plymouth Country Club and helps me appreciate it even more. I love to travel and build new experiences but am always happy to come home to the course where my heart is.

THE 19TH HOLE

19th Hole (A)

FAVORITE 19TH HOLES

The following is a list of our favorite 19th Holes in golf. We have been fortunate to have visited multiple post golf watering holes but are always looking for the next one. These are in random order because it is impossible to call one better than the others.

- **The Dunvegan, St Andrews Scotland:** Since the Old Course does not have a clubhouse that most can get into, this is a great pub to visit as it is only a "9 Iron" away from the 18th green. Good pub food with a mix of golfers and locals.

- **The Jigger Inn, St Andrews Scotland:** Used to be where the caddies went after their round, but we did not see any when we visited. We sat outside on a warm summer night, and it was entertaining to watch groups hit their second shots into the 17th Road Hole Green. Basic pub food and we enjoyed the short walk out to it from our hotel, Rusacks.

- **Salem Country Club, Peabody, MA:** The outside patio is the perfect place for a post round beverage and to watch groups finish on 18. Great outdoor space and always love sitting here. On colder days Salem has the Ross Room which has an old-time pub feel to it.

- **Sticks at Spanish Bay, Pebble Beach, CA:** Tina and I loved Sticks as it was the perfect place to relax, enjoy the ocean view and watch football after golf. We watched the Patriots beat the Baltimore Ravens here in a great playoff game. Spanish Bay has another one of our favorites, the Fire Pit area. A wonderful place for a drink at sunset and to see and hear the bagpiper come out of the sand dunes. This spot has been mentioned in a couple of my prior stories.

- **The Deuce at Pinehurst, NC:** Good food, beer and a splendid view of the groups finishing on the 18th at the famous Pinehurst #2 course. If you make a "2" on any of the par threes at #2, make sure to take your card to the bar and get your commemorative ball marker. Sadly, we did not get one, but one of our playing partners did! He was a member and told us about this tradition.

- **The Patio and Bar at Taconic Golf Club, Williamstown, MA:** Tina and I enjoyed sitting out on the patio and watching groups finish on the par 5 18th hole. A scenic spot overlooking the mountains, and if it is too hot, the old style inside bar is welcoming too.

- **In the Rough Lounge, Pine Needles Golf Course, Southern Pine, NC:** Beautiful old-style sunken bar and large comfortable chairs. Great food, nice outside deck and we always meet interesting people at the bar. Always skilled bartenders too who make a stellar cocktail. The burger here is outstanding.

- **The Ryder Cup Bar, Kiawah, Island, SC:** Great place to sit on a lovely day and watch groups finish on 18 of the Ocean Course. If you get a cold windy day like we did a few years ago in March, the inside bar works well too. On that cold March day, Tina experienced having her first ever Scotch to warm up after the round. We had better luck with the weather on our first visit a few years earlier in September. It was a sunny and warm day, and we sat outside and enjoy the view with lunch looking out at the ocean and the finishing hole. Fantastic way to celebrate our anniversary!

- **East Lounge at the North Berwick Golf Club, Berwick, Scotland:** The club could not have been nicer with the general manager greeting us after we finished 18 and inviting us into their lovely clubhouse for lunch. Food was delicious and wish we had made it to the upstairs balcony to see the view down the 18th hole back towards the ocean. We loved the hospitality at this place and want to return.

- **Hollins House at Pasatiempo Golf Course, Santa Cruz, CA:** One of my favorite golf courses and we were glad we discovered the Hollins House after we completed our round. It was the perfect place to kill some time before our red eye flight home. This is a finer dining experience than you would find at most golf courses. We found a spot at the bar that had a magnificent view of the Pacific Ocean behind us and a tasty meal before heading home.

- **Rusacks Dining Room, St. Andrews, Scotland:** There have been changes and expansion at Rusacks since we have been there, but this spot was a favorite of ours for breakfast as you can watch all the groups heading down the first fairway of the Old Course. Not a 19th hole, but one of the best places we have ever gone to start our day.

- **Ardglass Golf Club, Ardglass, Northern Ireland:** The mere fact that the clubhouse is a former castle and is the oldest clubhouse in the world (900-year-old castle!) makes it necessary for this list. They serve pub style food inside the castle. A good place to get warm, and I remember having a hearty soup after playing on a wet and raw day.

- **Hyannisport Golf Club, Hyannisport, MA:** They have so many spots now to sit but we love the upstairs bar in the cooler months, where the view and sunset is the best on Cape Cod. Our friends who are members say, "why do we need an ocean front home when we have a place to come with this view." The new outside fire pit area is nice too.

- **Old Head Golf Club, The Terrace, and Lusitania Bar, Kinsale, Ireland:** Great views of the lighthouse and 18th hole from The Terrace at Old Head. A bit on the expensive side but we got engaged here and the food was delicious. Caddies congregate at the **Speckled Hen Pub** right down the road after their loops. Our caddie Mickie invited us to stop down, and we always wish we did.

- **Mauna Lani Golf Club, Kohala Coast, Big Island Hawaii:** Not the busiest place (we visited in September during the slow season), but it has a nice open-air bar with views to the ocean and Maui. Cool breezes and delicious drinks. A good combination.

- **The Lodge at Torrey Pines:** Comfortable outdoor seating and no better place to see a beautiful Pacific Ocean sunset looking out over the golf course. Perfect food, drinks, and atmosphere to relax after golf.

- **Plymouth Country Club, Plymouth, MA:** Our home club with a sweet view of the ocean and Plymouth Bay from the deck. A beautiful spot to have a cocktail and watch the sunset.

19th Hole (B)

FAVORITE 19TH HOLE STORIES

CARNOUSTIE, SCOTLAND:

Tina and I had just finished our round at the famous Carnoustie Golf Links in Scotland. It was an unusual day in Scotland with the temperature a warm, eighty-five degrees. Being we were there in the summer, we did better than the locals at coping with the heat. Our caddies struggled, and the temperature was substantially above what was normal for them. At one point I thought my caddie was going to pass out. He was looking weak and was searching for water on every hole.

The final three holes at Carnoustie are as difficult as any final three we have ever played. The 16th is a long par 3 of 220 yards followed by two brutally long par fours with the Barry Burn winding between the holes.

The Burn was in play on every shot on the last few holes, and it was made famous in 1999 by Frenchman Jean Van De Velde who threw away his chance to be the first Frenchman to win The Open since 1908. Van De Velde had a three-shot lead standing on the 18th tee and only needed to play conservatively to win. What followed was a disaster for Van De Velde, who made a series of poor decisions and needed to make an eight-foot putt just to make a playoff with Paul Laurie. Laurie went on to win the playoff in what is remembered as one of the saddest and bizarre finishes in Open history.

Those last few holes beat us up, and we decided it might be good to have a quick drink and cool down, before making the short trek back to St Andrews.

The obvious place for a drink was the large white building behind the 18th green. You always see it in the TV broadcasts of The Open from Carnoustie, but I had read marginal reviews of the place just prior to our trip. We decided to look for an alternative but were struggling to find a place.

A caddie who had been working in the group playing in front of us was coming in our direction. We did not know the area so we stopped him and asked if he knew of a place where we could have a drink. He was kind and said to us, follow me, my club is right across the street. It turned out to be the Carnoustie Golf Club. The club's current building was built in 1898, and according to their website, the club is the 10th oldest golf club in the world.

What good fortune for us. We walked across the street to his clubhouse. He gave us a tour and proudly told us the history of the club and showed us the metals and trophies members had won at various competitions. There were pictures of Ben Hogan, who made his one appearance at The Open at Carnoustie and won it in 1953.

Our host then said to us that with the heat we must be thirsty. He took us up to the bar and introduced us to the bartender and bought us each a pint. This was unexpected and so kind!

Being parched and a bit overheated, we were glad to have drinks and cool down. We then told our host we were attending The Open the next day and could see it was now on TV in the club. Our new friend set us up at a table with a view of the TV so we could enjoy our drinks and watch the action from Muirfield. It was different to watch it because it was the BBC feed, not the normal coverage we get in the US.

Our new friend then told us he would love to have a pint with us, but he needed to get home. He told us to stay as long as we wanted and made sure the bartender knew that we were his guest. Unfortunately, we never got his name but his kindness to a couple of lost looking Americans is something we will never forget.

KINGSBARNS, SCOTLAND:

Kingsbarns is one of the most beautiful courses we have played in Scotland, and we were looking forward to playing it for a second time during our vacation. We arrived early to take advantage of their outstanding practice facility and headed to the first tee to see who we would be paired with.

To our surprise, when we got closer to the tee there were three people waiting for us. It was a bit of a mystery, but we learned quickly that only two were playing golf.

Our partners for this day were a Scottish family. A grandfather, father, and son. They had driven over two hours to play Kingsbarns, and the son had given the round of golf to his dad for his birthday. The granddad had come to walk along and be with the boys when they played the round. Something you rarely see in the US, since the courses in the US want a cart guest fee for this. Not so in Scotland where strolling along is encouraged.

Both dad and son were skilled players and clearly the grandfather enjoyed walking along, seeing this scenic course, and watching his boy's play. Both father and son hit the ball a long way and we enjoyed playing with them.

As we were shaking hands and getting ready to sadly leave the 18th green, our new friends enquired on what are plans were after golf. Being on vacation and staying in nearby St Andrews, we said just heading back to town was our plan. This plan changed quickly when our new friends invited us to join them for a post round pint.

What followed was a lively two hours where we had not one but two pints and talked about multiple subjects. The discussion ranged from politics in Scotland, to life in America, and questions about the large US cities like New York and Boston. We discussed their feelings about who they liked in the upcoming Open Championship. We learned an interesting lesson about the Scots from this.

Being in the British Isles, I asked our new Scottish friends who they would be pulling for in The Open, Justin Rose, Lee Westwood, or Ian Poulter? I knew by the looks on their faces that I had made a mistake.

The young son replied, "hell no, I would not want any of them to win, they are all English. We would rather see one of our own from Scotland win, or Tiger, or Phil Mickelson." I touched a nerve, and it was clear that centuries old feelings still ran deep.

Luckily, they quickly forgave my erroneous assumption, and we continued the discussion till the second pint was finished.

They asked us to stay for one more pint, but we had to navigate the winding road back to town driving on the wrong side of the road. Even though we were tempted, we thought better of the offer and headed back to our hotel.

It made us sad to leave but it was a wonderful day with perfect weather and interesting company. It was a memorable and enjoyable 19th hole experience.

INN AT SPANISH BAY, PEBBLE BEACH, CA:

My company ran an incentive trip for our customers to help increase production. The trip destination for the winners was to the world-famous Pebble Beach golf resort. For extra motivation, our manager told us that if we had customers who qualified we could go along on the trip. Needless to say, I worked hard and was motivated to get my customers on the trip. Four of my customers qualified, including my good friend Steve Roy.

Steve and I decided to play a warmup round once we arrived at Spanish Bay, and we headed off by taxi to the Bayonet and Blackhorse courses over in nearby Seaside, CA. This is a fine 36-hole public complex that used to be on a military base and had now been made public. The greens fees were much more reasonable than Pebble Beach or any of the other courses in the Pebble Beach stable.

After the round, we met our fellow travelers at the firepits at Spanish Bay. A perfect spot for a pre-dinner cocktail. As mentioned in a prior story, every evening at dusk a bagpiper comes out of the sand dunes next to the fire pits to play for the group gathered. We arrived just in time to witness this, and we ordered drinks.

Steve, being more sophisticated than me, was looking for something tastier than your average 19th hole beer. He enquired what the server would recommend for a Cabernet Sauvignon.

Being that Spanish Bay is a Five Star rated resort to no surprise the cabernet they served him was outstanding.

It was so good that Steve ordered this cabernet at every meal and 19th hole gathering for the balance of the trip. He enjoyed it and before we left wanted to make sure he got the name right so he could track it down and enjoy it again at home.

Lo and behold when he took a look at the menu, he realized that he had been enjoying a fine Silver Oak Cab, and it was $28 a glass! A tad more than the Bud Lights the others in the group had been drinking.

I know Steve was a little taken aback by the price. There was certainly a good lesson learned on this trip though. First check the price of what you are ordering and then be glad someone else is paying!

TACONIC GOLF CLUB, WILLIAMSTOWN, MA:

Taconic is one of our favorite golf courses in MA and this trip was one of the best golf adventures that Tina and I have taken. The trip started with a visit to Lee, MA to play a 9-hole course designed by Donald Ross called Greenock. It was busy with the club championship starting right after we teed off, but it was pleasurable to play.

Following our round, we checked in a short way up the road at the Williams Inn. After a quick rest we headed back down the road to Tanglewood to see the Boston Pops and Kristin Chenoweth perform. Ms. Chenoweth is one of Tina's favorite actresses. She is best known for being the orig-

inator of the role of Glinda the Good Witch in the musical
Wicked. She is tiny, but she can sure belt out a tune.

After a good night's sleep, day two started with a trip to
the Clark Museum at Williams College. I am not the most
artsy guy, but we enjoyed this and were able to see their two
special exhibits, the original painting of Whistler's Mother
and a collection of works by Vincent Van Gogh. This filled
our morning before we headed over to finish the trip with
a round at beautiful Taconic Golf Club. On the campus
and owned by Williams College, it is one of the best public
courses in our state.

As usual when we travel in a twosome, it is always interesting to see with whom we get paired with. This day our
pairing was with a woman named Olivia and her friend
Nick.

The first surprise of the round was when we went to tee
it up. Olivia played from the same tees as Nick and me. She
said her dad had always made her play from the same tees
with him and she was comfortable with it. After seeing her
first drive there was no doubt, she was more than comfortable.

It was a sweltering hot day and Olivia and Nick decided
to walk. We decided to take a cart. The heat and humidity
was building, and the cart looked like a safer option. Towards the end of the round, you could see the heat had tak-
en its toll on all of us but especially our new partners who
walked and carried their golf bags the entire round.

We were glad to see the 18th green and the old-style
clubhouse not far behind it. Normally we would have opted
to be outside on their patio, but the heat made the inside
seating a logical choice this day.

We ordered beers and food and had a nice post round conversation. Nick and Olivia wanted to find a swimming hole that Nick visited as a kid, and we had a long ride back to Hanover. Tina and I got up to hit the locker room for a quick rinse and to freshen up.

When we returned, our partners for the day were not at the table. They left a note saying they were sorry to leave in such a hurry, but they were afraid they would not find the swimming hole after sunset.

The server then came by, and we asked if we could settle our part of the check. The server smiled and gave us surprising news. She let us know that our new friends had told her they had a fun day with us, and they had taken care of the bill.

It again goes to show how you meet generous people through golf.

This would be a remarkable story if it ended here but sometimes life takes strange twists.

One morning a few years later, I was sitting at our kitchen table reading the Sunday Boston Globe. As I was searching for the sports section, a picture on the back page of another section caught my eye. It was a featured picture of two newlyweds. When I looked closer, I realized it was our golf partners, Nick, and Olivia, from Taconic. A small world story for sure.

Through family we had a connection who knew Nick and were able to secure his contact info.

We sent Olivia and Nick a wedding card, including a thank you note for their kindness for treating us to lunch at Taconic. We included a wedding gift. It was an offer to host them for a round of golf at our home club, Plymouth Country Club.

We received a heartfelt reply from them and set up a date to meet. With bad luck, the weather did not cooperate on the date we picked, and we had to cancel our golf. It was disappointing but it was fun to reconnect with them.

We did try to reschedule but life had become busier for our golf friends. They both have demanding careers and a growing family. Hopefully, one of these days we will meet again and play!

APPENDIX

Appendix #1

12 POINT GUIDE FOR SUCCESSFUL BUSINESS GOLF

I was fortunate to have a job for years that afforded me the opportunity to play many rounds of business golf with my customers. I received training on every part of my job but got little instruction or help on how to manage being in this type of a business situation.

The only advice I received from one senior executive was not helpful. His advice was if you play any business golf with a customer, always let the customer win. I know the customers I played with would not agree with this and it was advice I never followed. Letting the customer win all the time could be an expensive strategy, and I am not sure my customers would respect me for going in the tank for them.

Thinking about that comment about letting the customer win made me think it would be helpful to share what I have learned over thirty years of playing business golf.

1. **Get a USGA handicap:** It is an easy thing to do, and you can get one at any public club for around $35 a year. It shows you are serious about the game; and if you are invited to a member/guest tournament, you

will need an official handicap, or many clubs will have you play at scratch.

2. **Expect to be nervous:** Playing business golf is different than playing with your friends. You may be playing with someone for the first time and someone you do not know well. It is a fantastic opportunity to spend 4-6 hours with a person or group in a business situation that you normally would not get. I would tell people that if I had a meeting with the CEO or any high-ranking executive of my company it would last a short time, likely less than a half hour. Business golf is a terrific way to get access to people who would not normally give you that much of their time.

3. **Arrive early:** It seems like common sense, but I have seen people show up right at the tee time. Arrive early and get situated, get warmed up and be ready to go when you are on the tee. "Trunk Slamming" is rude and shows a lack of understanding and respect of how things work in golf.

4. **Have a plan for the visit:** What are you looking to accomplish with the round of golf? Build a relationship, close a deal, make a new connection? Know what you want to achieve with the day and your investment of time will be well worth it.

5. **Stay off your phone:** All clubs have different policies regarding cell phones. Check with your host beforehand on what the club policy is. The best idea is to put the phone away for the four hours you are playing. If

you cannot dedicate the time to be offline, you may be better off not playing.

6. **Understand who you are playing with and where you are playing:** I have played with a diverse group of golfers during my career. From those who were happy to play a scramble to those who played in higher-level Mass Golf and USGA events. It is easy to look up handicaps on GHIN.com and find out your host's handicap. It may help to know about the club and the club's history too. A Google search of the club's name will give you all the information you need and many course web-sites have details on the club's history.

7. **Know the rules:** An embarrassing moment I remember well is when a guest I brought decided he was going to play preferred lies no matter where his ball was. Our host was a serious player and was taken back by this breach of etiquette. The host asked me not to bring this person back again. An easy rule to follow is to not touch your ball until you can mark it on the putting green. If in doubt or if it is wet, ask if the group is playing lift clean and place or playing the ball up. Asking your playing partners on any situation is always a safe way to go.

8. **Bring cash:** Every time I was invited, there was some kind of game. One of my clients taught me early on that golf bets are sacred and need to be paid. It can be tricky if someone decides to not pay, but if I was on the losing end of the match, I always paid up. It is bad form to make a bet then "forget" to pay. Bets should be settled as soon as you sit down after the round. Sure,

you can use Venmo these days, but cash is always better. I cannot say that I was paid after every match I have played. In most cases I was playing a fine course, during a workday, for no cost, but I always remember the people who reneged on their bets.

9. **Be available to stay after:** I have heard repeatedly the old saying "business is done on the golf course." I do not agree with this. On the course is a place where relationships are built but it is not the correct place for serious business discussions. After golf is the perfect opportunity for more serious discussions. The round is over, bets are settled, everyone is more relaxed and now there is sufficient time to focus on business without the interruptions that take place on the golf course. Throughout my career multiple deals were consummated when we sat down after the round and hashed out the details.

10. **Know when it is time to go:** All good things must end, and it is the same for a day on the golf course. It can be tempting to stay but better to leave a little early than overstay your welcome and have one more beverage.

11. **Send a written thank you note:** It is now a lost art, but there is no way to make a better impression than sending a personal, handwritten thank you note. Doing this always makes a good impression and is more personal than an email or text.

12. **Make a follow up visit with a gift:** I always took advantage of this opportunity to stop by my client's office

with a small gift for the day of golf. I would often deliver the written thank you note at the same time. This puts a nice cap on the event and showed I valued what my client did for me. Sometimes the gift was a shirt, golf balls or company swag. Frequently after doing this, I would hear the statement, "appreciated but not necessary." That statement made me always think what I did was correct and could help me get invited back again!

You can learn a great deal about someone on the golf course. "Listen with your eyes" is one of the best pieces of advice I ever received. Watching how someone treats the golf course, caddies, and staff can give you valuable insight about that person. Same with how they act on the course. Do they care for the course, fix ball marks and divots, and play by the rules? Are they humble in victory and gracious in defeat? Actions on the golf course can teach you quite a bit about a person and their values and character.

Golf is a terrific way to spend time with your clients and learn more about them. To me, there is no better way to build your relationship with a client. It is an effective way to have fun and fresh air during a workday.

Good luck, swing easy and play well!

Appendix #2

BUSINESS GOLF: EXPERIENCES AND LESSONS

In the prior chapter I wrote about a "12 Point Guide for Successful Business Golf." There were multiple experiences over thirty years of playing business golf that shaped these reasons. For me, my motivation was simple. The majority of my clients belong to wonderful places to play, and I wanted to earn the chance to play these courses. I realized I could build better relationships with my clients through golf. The following are examples of learning experiences I had through golf, which taught me much about life, business, and people.

FIRST BUSINESS INVITE

My eyes were opened early in my marketing career by a client who at first, I did not care for. Our business discussions tended to be confrontational, and my company (and I) were frustrated with the overall relationship with his large insurance agency. I did not enjoy my visits with him, and we had a tough time finding common ground. One day I noticed a book about Donald Ross on his desk. As usual, our business discussion was not going well, so I figured I had nothing to lose by asking about the book.

For the next half hour, I did not speak. We had found something my client was much more interested in talking about than insurance. It was golf, and his passion for Donald Ross golf courses.

At this point I did not know a Ross from a Raynor. This day I learned the difference. We had a long discussion about the Ross courses in New England and the Donald Ross Society of which he was an active member. He gave me a list of Ross courses that I still have today, which had all the Ross designed courses in the Northeast. He said he had played about 90% of them and challenged me to try to play all of them. I have not reached 90% but I have played 75% of the Ross courses in MA.

He told me about his relationship with one of our competitors and how through them he had been able to play the Ross courses in our area. The people who held my job at this company had memberships at many of the best of these Ross courses and he was a regular guest. He told me he was a frequent invitee because he was always willing to move his schedule around when they needed a person at the last minute, and he knew how to "play the game." Simply, he knew how to be a good guest.

The discussion certainly went a long way to improving our relationship and I actually looked forward to the visits because I knew there would always be a new story or adventure for him to tell me about. Most importantly was the improved business relationship which put me on the list for the agency's annual series of golf outings. At these outings they entertained key company people at the lovely private Ross course where my contact was a member. I could not have been more excited due to this being my first real invite to a business golf event.

The event lived up to my lofty expectations. My contact organized three four-man teams that would play against each other. There was a twenty dollar buy in, and multiple ways to win. I played competitively and my host was impressed when I drove the ball farther than anyone in my group. It was good to play well, even if I did not fully understand all the different "games" going on.

It was a sweltering day, and we were all happy to finish our round. We retired to the air-conditioned grill room for libations. The Foster's Lager beer waiting for us never tasted so good.

After a couple cold ones, we headed upstairs to the dining room to a delicious steak and seafood dinner. The cash from the day's contests was doled out and our host had shirts laid out from the pro shop on a piano for each of us to take. We won cash, I picked out a nice shirt, and played a great old course. Quite an event and even better, our business relationship improved more after this day.

Not every outing was like this, though. Most were much lower key and normally it would be only four people. The following year, I was invited to another one and learned a good lesson about being on time.

EARLY BIRD GETS THE WORM

This time I was playing with one of my managers and we received instructions to be at the golf course at 9:30 am sharp. We met in the parking lot at 9:20. Immediately when we arrived one of our hosts hustled over to us and gave us startling news. Our other host was on the tee and waiting for us. We hurried to get our shoes on and rushed up the stairs to the tee. My manager almost took a tumble on the stairs as he had not tied his shoes. He stumbled up the stairs and was lucky to save himself from falling. He already had a tender back, and this rushing was not helping.

After a little good-natured ribbing on the tee about rushing us and trying to win the match before it had even started (it was done for exactly that reason), we took a couple of practice swings and off we went. At that moment I decided this would never happen again when visiting someone else's club. I decided I would always arrive at least 45 minutes early.

A LESSON IN BAD MANNERS

It is always interesting to see someone's behavior away from their employees and office. It has been said you can learn a great deal by playing golf with someone, but I believe you can learn a good deal about someone by sharing a meal with them too. I could not believe what took place at another fine metro Boston golf club when another client of mine invited me there.

The person who invited me had talked extensively about golf during our business meetings, and he belonged to two fine golf clubs. One club was near his office in MA and the other near his vacation home in NH. He talked a good game, and he extended an invite for lunch followed by golf a few weeks later.

As we sat down for lunch, I was taken aback by how he spoke to our younger college-age server. While his office was run efficiently, I never saw any disrespect shown to his employees. Not the case here; and when our server brought out his clam chowder, my host screamed at her that she needed to take it back right now as it was not hot enough. When I say screamed, it was so loud everyone in the crowded dining room turned their eyes toward our table. It was uncomfortable for every person in the room, and I could feel the disapproving stares being shot at our table.

I felt sorry for our server and embarrassed by my client's rude actions. It was just so over the top and unnecessary and I could never imagine treating someone this rudely. My host exited the dining room before me to change into golf clothes, and I had the chance to slip over and apologize to her. She thanked me for stopping by and ducked quickly into the kitchen.

We headed for the golf course and things did not get better. My host told me that he did not have many people at the club that would play with him (not shocking after the lunch encounter) and he was not a particularly skillful player. He delivered on that description right away on the first hole with a ground ball off the tee. It was a good thing we were a twosome, and the course was not busy. It was quickly clear this was going to be a long and painfully slow round.

I was happy and relieved when the round was over. It made me realize that even a top-notch golf course could not make up for second rate behavior and terrible play.

HIGH STAKES MATCH

Most times there was some kind of match involved with my business golf invites. The majority were friendly and for small stakes. The most money you could win or lose would be ten to twenty dollars. Two and five-dollar Nassau bets (a standard golf bet with three matches in one). This day, the stakes got pushed significantly higher and was a match I will never forget.

On this occasion, I was a guest of a high-profile client whom I had played with before. For an unknown reason, on this day, he decided that we were going to double the normal bet. Since money was no problem for him, the higher stakes were no issue. Not the case for me. I was not accustomed to larger stakes golf gambling games.

Since I was a guest, I had no choice in the stakes and my partner told me to relax and treat it like it was just another match. I listened to him, but I still had the thought in my head that if things went really badly, I could lose more money than I had in my wallet. That would be embarrassing.

I am sure these are exactly the thoughts our host wanted me to have. No doubt, pushing me out of my comfort zone was what he planned to do. A wise old golf saying says most matches are not won or lost on the course, they are won and lost in the negotiations on the first tee.

The match was a good one and our team won the front nine by one hole. The back was more up and down and there were a few presses (press is doubling of the bet) open so the stakes got up to a much higher level.

The match came down to the 18th hole which was a slight dog leg left. We were playing on a late fall day and had started later than we had planned, so we were playing the final hole at sunset.

Our team had the honor, and my partner and I both hit good drives. Our opponents followed and neither hit a good one. The first one was short and high. The second one, hit by our high-profile host, headed to the woods on the right side of the hole. With the sun now low in the sky, it was hard to see where his offline shot had ended up.

The high-profile guy shot off like a cannon after his ball. My partner and I trailed behind and he headed to his ball which was more left than mine. Our opponent had now reached the woods and had started the search for his ball. I was the closest player to him and started to walk through the rough towards the woods to help him find the ball. When I got closer to him, I heard "I got it." Miraculously, his ball landed in an opening with a clear shot to the green.

Just when I was returning to my ball, I noticed a ball sitting down deep in the rough. Since he had found his ball, I bent over and picked this one up. I was certainly surprised by what I saw.

The ball I found had a logo on it, and it was the logo of the high-end guy's company. This was either the greatest coincidence ever or he had decided to drop a ball to give him a chance to win the hole.

What I think happened was in the dim light none of us saw how the ball ended up. It either did not go as far as he thought, or it hit a tree and bounced back into the rough. Whatever happened I now had a conundrum. Do I call this large client out and risk the fallout, or play on and just try to win the hole? Not an easy decision given my position and what was at risk for my company and me.

In the end, I decided to play it out and just try to win.

I hit my shot onto the green and it was about thirty feet from the hole. His shot out of the woods was closer, about ten feet. It was quite a shot and now the pressure was on me to get down in two and make a par.

I putted first and left the putt about four feet short. Not the putt I was looking for and it was far enough away I was going to have to make it. Given the match was on the line there was no way the putt would be conceded. The other two guys were out of the hole, so it was now the high-end guy who now had his chance for birdie and the win. His putt just missed and was only about three inches from the hole. This was close enough for it to be conceded.

That left it all up to me and I would need to make the 4-footer for our side to have a big win. Multiple thoughts were going through my mind, too many about what I should have done back in the fairway. I stepped up to the putt and jabbed at it quickly and it slid by the hole. It was the most expensive putt I had ever missed. We had won a little money, but it would have been twice the payout if I had made the putt.

We shook hands and I knew we had missed a big score but was relieved the match was over. It made me think about the old Vince Lombardi quote, "winning isn't everything, it's the only thing." In this case, having the chance to cut his losses was overly important to my host, but his actions certainly seemed out of line. Being out of my comfort zone was not easy but I certainly learned from the experience.

I wondered why someone with more money than they could ever spend in a lifetime, would resort to dropping a ball like I think he did. I guess I will never know the answer, but my best guess is there are people who just have to win no matter what the cost.

I kept the ball for a long time as a reminder of what took place. Our business relationship changed soon after this, and I was happy to move on.

LAST MINUTE DROPOUTS

During my career I would run golf tournaments for my company's customers. I loved doing it and it was a challenge to pair the correct people together to get the maximum business value from the event for all parties. While I loved doing this, every tournament had the same challenge, late cancellations.

I heard every excuse in the book and I am sure a few of the excuses were legitimate. I was always amazed at how good clients would not take the commitment to attend seriously and think nothing of calling even hours before the event to bow out. Having been on the side of organizing an event, I do not remember any time I bowed out of an event I was invited to at the last minute.

It is just bad form.

CLOSING

What are the lessons learned from my business golf? For me it was that overall business golf was a great tool and a perfect way to get to know clients better. In every case, there would be no way to get four plus hours of time with any of these people in their respective offices. There is nothing more valuable than someone's time, and golf gave me more of it with my key people, certainly more than any other business activity I did with my clients.

Like many things in life, business golf does have pitfalls and things can go wrong. I was glad for all the great experiences but certainly realized there could be risks to the relationships if you were not careful. Not a reason not to participate and play, just a reason to be on guard and realize that things can happen that you would not anticipate.

Relax, play hard and have fun!

Appendix #3

FAVORITE FAIRWAY FINDS

We love to find places that are off the beaten path. Before the internet and the enormous amount of info available with Google, I would have called these courses hidden gems. I am not sure there are hidden gems anymore, so we went with our own title, Favorite Fairway Finds.

This list contains places we have enjoyed for a different reason than just a name or ranking. Most offered a "unique" experience. Ironically, more than a few are located quite close to a more famous course.

- **Greenock Country Club, Lee, MA** This is a 9-hole course right on the way to the more well-known Berkshire neighboring course, Taconic. It was in tip-top shape and a pleasure to play the day we visited. A little tight in places when it is busy, but given that it is a rare Ross 9-hole course it was a good stop on the way to Williamstown and Taconic

- **Chequessett Yacht and Country Club and Highlands Links, Wellfleet and Truro MA:** Two old time classics as far out as you can find golf courses on Cape Cod. They will not break the bank budget wise, and Highland Links is as close as you will get to links golf on the Cape Cod coast. If you are up for three in one day, start off at Chatham Seaside Links, right next to the iconic Chatham Bars Inn.

- **Marion Golf Course, Marion, MA:** Most speed right by it on the way to its top one hundred neighbor Kittansett. New owners have done work to take down trees and open up the original design by George Thomas (of Riviera fame). A favorite of the hickory golf set, it offers a variety of holes with a couple of holes protected by rock walls. The cost to play it is reasonable and it is easy to walk.

- **Pasatiempo, Santa Cruz, CA:** It is a perfect stop on the way to or from Pebble Beach; and even though it is highly rated, I am always surprised people have not heard of it when I suggest a stop there to play. It is one of the few Alister Mackenzie designed courses that is public. The price has gone up, but I would still go back and play it again. It does have an Augusta National feel to it, and we felt one hole looked much like the eighteenth at the Masters. The Hollins House located on a hill behind the first tee is a great spot to stop for a delicious meal. We sat at the bar and enjoyed the view and quality food before our red eye flight back to Boston.

- **Ardglass, Ardglass Northern Ireland:** We played here the day after we played Royal County Down. An excellent value considering it cost as much for the foursome to play as it cost for one player at RCD. An enjoyable course to play with impressive scenery along the seacoast. The clubhouse is a 900-year-old castle and the oldest clubhouse in the world. Most drive right on by it to its more famous neighbors, but I know our group would go back here in a minute.

- **Annesley Links Newcastle, Northern Ireland:** Located on the same land where its more famous neighbor Royal County Down is located, it is a much shorter and easier course than the championship course. We found it fun to play with a mix of shorter par four holes and par threes. The middle holes from four to sixteen were a perfect mix of short and longer distances and challenging to play. My son Erik and I played it late in the day and played it in just over two hours. Most rush by it to get to the big course, but if I could do it again, I would play this one as a warmup.

- **Cavendish Golf Course Lanai City, Hawaii:** The most unique place I have ever played. It is a free golf course located right next to the Four Seasons Hotel on Lanai. Built by Dole Pineapple for their workers back in the day when they dominated the island, it is golfing the old-fashioned way. The fairways were not lush but there were challenging holes that would fit well on any golf course. The day I played it, it was me and one other person on the course. Most island guests walk right by it and head to the Manele course down at the other Four Seasons location near the water. It was like a nature walk with golf clubs as it was peaceful and natural. Nobody cared what hole you started on or where you finished. I hope it survives the new owner of Lanai because it does not seem like it fits his upscale vision for the island.

- **The Glenn Golf Club, North Berwick, Scotland:** This was the first golf course my brother Mark and I played in Scotland. My first shot went a mile over the fence to the right. Once you climb the hill on the first hole you have a splendid view of Bass Rock and the ocean. It does not get the press and notice that some of their fine neighbors get (Muirfield, Gullane and North Berwick) but it was the perfect place to start on a Scotland trip and was an enjoyable walk.

- **Webhannett, Kennebunkport, ME:** I drove by a couple of the holes on this course for years and could never figure out where the clubhouse was located. This is a private course that opens up a few tee times a week to the public. We have played there after the season in early October. It is an old-style course and leisurely walk. Just make sure you confirm your tee time and price. Last time we played it during the summer, when we arrived at the pro shop, they had no record of our tee time. It was not busy, and thankfully they allowed us to play. It does not get the publicity of its neighbor Cape Arundel, but both are worth playing.

- **Bretwood Country Club Keene, NH:** For five years, I had to travel to Keene for work and every chance I would get I would head over here. Two underrated 18-hole public courses that are always in fine shape. The Ashuelot River meanders through both courses and does come into play. Bretwood does have a practice range too. If you are in the area, these two fine courses are worth a visit.

- **Laytown & Bettystown Links Golf Club Bettystown, Ireland:** It is wonderful that the great courses of Ireland and Scotland are open to public play. While it is nice you can play them, the price to play many of them has become prohibitive. To cut our cost when we traveled to Ireland, it meant finding courses like this one that are not as well known. Thanks to Tom Coyne's book "A Course Called Ireland" we found this place. It was not as tough as the top tier courses, but fun to play with many memorable holes. Our most fond memory was not about the course, but about the reception we received in the clubhouse after the round. Numerous members stopped at our table to speak with us and thanked us for choosing to play their course. No doubt their pride in their golf course was great and they all asked if we had enjoyed playing it. Over and over, we find courses like this provide an enhanced experience with their welcoming nature.

I'm sure everyone has their own gems, but these are a few of the ones we have enjoyed that are a little off the beaten path. Always good to find a bargain and we look forward to finding more places like these.

Appendix #4

ULTIMATE BUCKET LIST

have been fortunate to do plenty of fun things in golf but there is always more to do. Below is my current wish list. You can always dream!

- **Play at Cypress Point:** It may be a tough one, but I see people posting pictures all the time playing there. It may take some good luck, but it would be exciting to play the iconic 16th hole and the rest of this beautiful course.

- **Back-to-back days at National Golf Links of America and Shinnecock:** My son Erik says National is his favorite course. I would love to play this C.B. Mac-Donald gem and its more famous US Open host next-door neighbor.

- **Finish my goal to play every Donald Ross course in Massachusetts:** I have played 75% of them so far. I have been fortunate to played many of the top Ross courses but am missing Concord, Weston, Oakley, Pittsfield CC, and Longmeadow. I still have a few public ones to play but they should be easier to finish than the private ones.

- **Play every Donald Ross course in New England:** I am getting close in RI but have good ones to go like Point

Judith and Sakonnet. I have a longer way to go in Maine and New Hampshire but would love to play Bald Peak and Lake Sunapee.

- **Finish playing all the courses on the Cape and Islands:** Last year I finished all the courses on the Cape proper but have a way to go to get all the Island courses. The only one I have played so far on the islands is Farm Neck on Martha's Vineyard.

- **Spend a month in Scotland:** Love to spend a couple of weeks in St Andrews, then head over to Gullane and Berwick and then on to Royal Dornach and the Highlands.

- **Mid-Western Golf:** A gap in my courses played are the fine ones in Wisconsin. Sand Valley, Erin Hills, and Kohler may be too much for one stop, but I would love to play them all. They all look like outstanding resorts.

- **Best of Vermont:** A trip to Manchester, VT to play Ekwanok with Tina's cousin, Phil O'Rourke. A hidden gem for sure. The Equinox in that area looks sweet too.

- **A family golf adventure:** There are a bevy of attractive options. Love to find a way to get us all to Bandon, Sand Valley, or Scotland.

- **New Jersey to play Baltusrol:** We have been to the PGA there and this item will be dependent on my brother-in-law Kevin O'Rourke who has a family connection.

- **Complete playing all the courses designed by Mike Strantz:** I have played Tobacco Road, Bulls Bay,

True Blue, and Royal New Kent so far. Will play Caledonia in the spring of 2023. The tough one will be Monterey Peninsula CC where he did an amazing job on the Shore Course.

- **A Spring in Pinehurst**: So many courses and a months' time would allow the opportunity to explore more courses and re-play our favorites like Pine Needles and Mid-Pines.

- **Play golf in every state**: So far, I have played in twenty-six of fifty states. Still have a long way to go but a cross country trip could take care of many of the missing states.

- **Canada To Cabot**: If not for Covid we may have done this trip already. We have always wanted to go to Northern Maine so maybe a long two-week car trip to do this could work.

- **Golf in Norway:** Lofoten Links is one of the most northern golf courses in the world. I want to visit it and the country of Norway too.

- **Less traveled Ireland:** Up the Eastern shore to courses Enniscrone, County Sligo, Donegal and Narin & Portnoo These look like interesting courses and not as well traveled as the Southwest and Greater Dublin.

- **Attend Mike Bender Golf School:** Love his instruction on Instagram. His teaching methods are easy to understand.

- **Attend a Vision 54 Golf School:** A unique way of looking at golf instruction and concentrate more on the mental part of golf. Love their books, especially *Play Your Best Golf Now.*

- **Attend a "real" tournament round during the Masters:** We have been to a practice round, but it would be nice to see a "real" tournament round. We keep entering their ticket lottery but have not had any success since 2009.

- **Play Fisher Island Club and Yale Golf Course:** Love to play both of these Seth Raynor gems that are not that far away from our home.

- **Nebraska Golf:** The Prairie Club looks like quite a place and is public. This would be a real fun out of the way trip.

Appendix #5

MY PERSONAL TOP 99 COURSES PLAYED

I have had the good fortune of playing four hundred golf courses so far. I hope to add many more to this list in the coming years.

This list is my personal preference based on my experience from the day I played the course. The list does change from time to time as I play new courses and re-evaluate the experience at places I have played.

I am proud of the list and have lasting memories from the many top-notch courses I have had the pleasure of playing.

Name	Location
1. Pebble Beach	Pebble Beach, CA
2. Old Course	St Andrews, Scotland
3. Pacific Dunes	Bandon Dunes, OR
4. Royal County Down	Newcastle, Northern Ireland
5. Bethpage Black	Bethpage, NY
6. Kingsbarns Golf Links	Kingsbarns, Scotland
7. Bandon Dunes	Bandon Dunes, OR
8. The Country Club	Brookline, MA
9. The Ocean Course	Kiawah Island, SC
10. Pasatiempo	Santa Cruz, CA
11. North Berwick Golf Club	North Berwick, Scotland

12.	Waterville	Waterville, Ireland
13.	Lahinch	Lahinch, Ireland
14.	Bandon Trails	Bandon Dunes, OR
15.	Kittansett	Marion, MA
16.	Old MacDonald	Bandon Dunes, OR
17.	Old Sandwich	Plymouth, MA
18.	Streamsong Red	Bowling Green, FL
19.	Yeamans Hall Club	Hanahan, SC
20.	Portmarnock Golf Club	Dublin, Ireland
21.	Carnoustie	Carnoustie, Scotland
22.	Old Head Golf Links	Kinsale, Ireland
23.	Streamsong Blue	Bowling Green, FL
24.	Manele Golf Course	Lanai City, HI
25.	Pinehurst 2	Pinehurst, NC
26.	Chambers Bay	University Place, WA
27.	Taconic Golf Club	Williamstown, MA
28.	Sheep Ranch	Bandon Dunes, OR
29.	Essex Country Club	Manchester, MA
30.	Winchester CC	Winchester, MA
31.	Torrey Pines/South	La Jolla, CA
32.	Harbor Town	Hilton Head, SC
33.	Boston Golf Club	Hingham, MA
34.	Eastward Ho!	Chatham, MA
35.	Salem CC	Peabody, MA
36.	Wannamoisett CC	Rumford, RI
37.	Pine Needles	Southern Pines, SC
38.	Hyannisport	Hyannisport, MA
39.	Myopia Hunt Club	Hamilton, MA
40.	Tralee	Tralee, Ireland
41.	Newport CC	Newport, RI
42.	Gullane #1	Gullane, Scotland

43.	Plymouth CC	Plymouth, MA
44.	CC of Charleston	Charleston, SC
45.	Golden Horseshoe	Williamsburg, VA
46.	New Course	St Andrews, Scotland
47.	Mauna Kea	Waimea, HI
48.	Bay Hill Club	Orlando, FL
49.	Cog Hill #4	Lemont, IL
50.	Ballybunion	Ballybunion, Ireland
51.	Worcester CC	Worcester, MA
52.	Charles River CC	Newton, MA
53.	TPC Boston	Norton, MA
54.	Tobacco Road	Sanford, NC
55.	Ardglass	Ardglass, Northern Ireland
56.	Dormie Club	Pinehurst, NC
57.	Spanish Bay	Pebble Beach, CA
58.	Bulls Bay	Mt. Pleasant, SC
59.	True Blue	Pawley Island, SC
60.	Caledonia	Pawley Island, SC
61.	Spyglass Hill	Pebble Beach, CA
62.	Rhode Island CC	Barrington, RI
63.	TPC Sawgrass	Ponte Verde, FL
64.	Whitinsville CC	Whitinsville, MA
65.	Mid Pines	Southern Pines, SC
66.	Oyster Harbor Club	Osterville, MA
67.	Booth Bay Harbor Club	Boothbay, ME
68.	Wellesley CC	Wellesley, MA
69.	Sagamore Golf Course	Bolton Landing, NY
70.	Pinehill/Nicklaus	Plymouth, MA
71.	Carnegie Abby	Portsmouth, RI
72.	Experience at Koele	Lanai, HI
73.	Atlantic Dunes	Hilton Head, SC

74.	Turner Hill	Ipswich, MA
75.	Mauna Lani South	Waimea, HI
76.	Blue Hills CC	Canton, MA
77.	Belmont CC	Belmont, MA
78.	Sugarloaf Golf	Sugarloaf, ME
79.	Crump & Fox	Bernardston, MA
80.	Red Tail	Fort Devens, MA
81.	Mauna Lani North	Waimea, HI
82.	New Seabury/ Ocean	Mashpee, MA
83.	Pinehills/Jones	Plymouth, MA
84.	Farm Neck	Oak Bluffs, MA
85.	County Louth	Drogheda, Ireland
86.	Thorney Lea	Brockton, MA
87.	Woodland	Newton, MA
88.	Vesper	Tyngsboro, MA
89.	Cohasset CC	Cohasset, MA
90.	Cummiquid Golf Club	Yarmouth Port, MA
91.	Raven at 3 Peaks	Silverthorne, CO
92.	Club at Ravenna	Littleton, CO
93.	Warwick CC	Warwick, RI
94.	Bretwood	Keene, MA
95.	Richter Park	Danbury, CT
96.	The Orchards	South Hadley, MA
97.	George Wright	Hyde Park, MA
98.	Belgrade Lakes	Belgrade, ME
99.	The Ranch	Westfield, MA

Appendix #6

POSTSCRIPT

NOTES ABOUT THE AUTHOR

I hope you have enjoyed all 18 Chapters, plus the 19th Hole chapters, of Phil's "LIFE ABOVE PAR" golf tales. There are enough 19th hole stories to comprise a separate book. As a good friend of Phil's for 31 years, I have either participated, witnessed, or heard about these events during our frequent "Business Lunches." They are all factual without any embellishment.

I met Phil through the insurance business. He represented a major insurance company and called on our agency. It did not take long for us to become good friends and it quickly became obvious to me that golf was an important part of his life. At that time, I was an occasional golfer; however, with Phil's prodding, this did change.

All of us have difficulties in both our professional and personal lives. Phil is no different. Although I did not realize it at the time, I watched how golf helped him navigate the curves that life threw at him and kept him focused on the big picture.

I think that Mr. & Mrs. Phillip A. Robinson, Sr. knew what they were doing when they named their first-born son Phillip A. Robinson: initials PAR. Incredibly good initials for an avid golfer.

Falling off the ladder and severely injuring his elbow could have been a turning point either way. Phil was not about to give up. When he was able to return to limited golf, he struggled, and I know it worried him. I remember playing in his foursome at his Company's tournament in Plymouth MA. It was the only time in our friendship that I could beat him, due to the injury. That lasted a nanosecond as he started working his way back to becoming a low handicapper. I never did beat him again.

Phil retired from a successful insurance career on April 30, 2021. Needless to say, he is playing as much golf as his body and time will allow. I am sure he is also collecting more experiences and someday down the road we just might see a sequel to "LIFE ABOVE PAR."

On a personal note, when Phil was nearing the end of drafting the book and we were enjoying lunch and an adult beverage he asked if I would write the Epilogue. Naturally, I was honored. However, I was also intimidated at the same time. I am sure there were others he could have chosen, but I am thankful for the opportunity.

Roy Eaton
Friend and Mentor

Appendix #7

ACKNOWLEDGEMENTS

In starting a project like this one, I had no conception of the time and effort it would take to put together this book. There is no doubt that it would not have happened without the efforts and support of my wife, Tina Robinson.

Tina's spirit of optimism and can-do attitude helped guide me through the ups and downs of the project. I am forever thankful for her patience and her tireless re-reading and editing of what I wrote. I could not have done it without her support, encouragement, and love!

Many thanks to my longtime friend Laura Nicholas for the time, effort, and suggestions she offered throughout the project. Always positive and always on point, Laura had constructive ideas on how to improve the writing. Laura took the picture that will grace the cover of this book on the day she, Tina and I played the beautiful Highland Links in Truro, MA. It is a perfect picture of a perfect golf day!

My good friends Rita and Roy Eaton were always willing to read my stories and give me feedback. Without them, any of the stories about Tina would not have happened. No doubt, "Cupid" did make the "*Match of A Lifetime*" and I appreciate their help and support.

Back fifteen years ago I met John Hopkins at Tina's 50th birthday celebration. We have enjoyed many dinners together, toasted with Makers Mark, and took a wonderful two week "retirement" vacation with him and his wife Kerry to Hawaii. John is a legendary English teacher and was the first one to read my book from start to finish. He gave me constructive feedback and pointed out "tics" in my writing style for me to correct. John was nice enough to do the reading and editing during his summer break from teaching. I may owe him at least another bottle of Makers Mark for his efforts and help.

Another English teacher that had great influence over me was Roy B. Merritt who taught at North Quincy High. Mr. Merritt brought entertainment, excitement, and engagement to his classes every day. He made us think, write, and try new things that sometimes made us uncomfortable. His was not a class you could show up and sleepwalk through. He brought it every day and expected you would too. Mr. Merritt passed away in 2009 at the age of 90 but I thought about him often while authoring this book.

Even though I have never met them, thanks to the golf writers and story tellers I have enjoyed reading over the years. Two whose stories I most enjoy are Tom Coyne, (*A Course Called Ireland* and many more) and George Peper who wrote one of my favorite books, "*Two Years in St. Andrews*." I love Mr. Peper's articles in Links Magazine, and I have incorporated many of his ideas into my own golf journey and bucket list.

I will never forget 9/11/22. But not for the normal memories we associate with 9/11. This was the date I woke up and was unable to see fully out of my left eye. Foolishly,

I attempted to play golf but realized quickly that something major was amiss with my sight since I was unable to track the golf ball. Since we have family history with eye issues, I spoke to my brother Mark who told me to head into Mass Eye and Ear Hospital as soon as possible.

Glad I did listen to Mark and am thankful for the outstanding care I received from the entire team at Mass Eye and Ear. A special thanks to my two surgeons, Dr. Nimesh Patel for repairing my detached retina and Dr. Shelia Borboli-Gerogiannis who performed my cataract surgery. It is amazing what they do every day.

The detached retina meant no golf or heavy lifting for two months. Again, good came from adversity, and I used the time to convert my rough draft into a final draft of this book. I am not sure the book would have been completed without the detached retina.

Lastly, thanks to all the people and places that made these stories possible. Without them, there would be no "LIFE ABOVE PAR!"

Feel free to leave comments and questions at the email address below. If you enjoyed the book, I would appreciate a review on the Amazon website!

Thanks again,
Phil Robinson (*parjr3388@gmail.com*)